From

NEWLYWED

to

FOREVERWED

A Guide to Preparing for Marriage
Like Planning for a Wedding

Stacey Steck

DEDICATION

This book is dedicated to those couples that have shown
the grace, wisdom, and courage that inspire others
to be better husbands and wives.

CONTENTS

Acknowledgments

Many people have been a part of the creation of this book. I am sincerely grateful to:

The members and Council of the Escazú Christian Fellowship in San José, Costa Rica for their faithfulness and for granting me the sabbatical during which this book was written;

Terrie Bennett and International Church Services, Inc. for generous funding that made the sabbatical possible;

Zdenek Patak and Rósa Valtingojer, coordinators of the Artist Residency program at the Here Creative Center in Stöðvarfjörður, Iceland, where the writing took place;

Those friends and colleagues who reviewed the earliest drafts and offered helpful and honest feedback;

Douglas DeFord for his friendship, consistent encouragement, and design of the book's cover;

Marnie Silbert for pointing me in the right direction to begin to understand marriage and family in a new way;

All the couples, whether engaged, married, or in crisis, that have shared their stories, opened their hearts, and trusted me with their hopes and fears;

And most of all, my wife, Flora Calderón-Steck, for many years of faithful partnership and the grace to allow me the time away to write this book while she stayed home with our precious small children, Julian and Lucia.

Part One

It's Not About You!

I suspect you will find that you won't have to wait until you are actually married to find the contents of this book to be helpful. You see, perhaps your biggest test is coming up: simply surviving your engagement and wedding!

If you are like most couples, you are entering one of the most stressful periods of your lives to date. The hyped-up culture and expectations around weddings, the positive and negative anxiety they arouse in families, and the frequent simultaneous planning of post-wedding practicalities (like where you will live, work, etc.) make the engagement period an emotional minefield. It is no wonder it is a staple of Hollywood tragi-comedies. We can all relate.

There will be times when you seriously think about leaving together for an intimate wedding with Elvis in Las Vegas. But when you have that feeling, here is what I want you to do: close your eyes, take a deep breath, and repeat (as many times as necessary), "It's not about me. It's not about me." When you grasp this simple fact about all weddings, yours will be fine too!

Yes, it is the two of you who are getting married, but the event has such wider implications. In addition to your own expectations for your new life together, everyone else has theirs too! Your parents are depending on you for grandchildren. Your boss can't wait for the wedding to be over so you can once again give your full attention at work. The institution of marriage, and thus all of human civilization, is at the point of collapse. Your pastor wants you to be a shining example of the church's brilliant pre-marital preparation program. Not to be too dramatic about it but there's not a lot of room for error here, people!

But you just want to get married.

Weddings are one of what you could call life-cycle events, those circleable moments or events on the calendars of our lives like the losing of your first tooth or your virginity, graduation from high school or college, first communion or confirmation in the church, the birth of a child, the death of a parent or grandparent, a divorce – whatever marks a transition from one status to another, one role to another, one way of looking at your life to another. We all have them, and because they tend to mean so much, they become opportunities for others to inject themselves into, and project themselves onto.

You see, none of these life-cycle events were only ever about you (unless you swallowed that tooth in the night and the tooth fairy never visited your house). There has always been someone else involved who had a significant stake in that moment of your life. Your life-cycle events meant as much or more to them as they did to you. Your wedding will be no different. And that means challenges for you.

Here are just a few reasons, none of which have to do directly with you, why the months leading up to your wedding could be an anxious time for you:

- Feelings about the state of other people's marriages aroused by your upcoming one.
- Fulfillment of parental dreams for a child's wedding

- The proximity of your wedding date to another significant life-cycle event or pivotal moments in one or both of your families (whether people are aware of it or not)
- Strained relationships between divorced (and possibly remarried) parents of the bride or groom
- Unresolved family conflicts in either family, or both
- Concerns (valid or not) that either set of future in-laws (or both!) has about the other family

And you, as the stars of the show, run the risk of receiving the lion's share of all the stress and anxiety experienced by those other people. If you let that happen.

The greatest temptation (consciously or unconsciously) will be for you to then redirect all that anxiety toward your beloved, where it will distill, in its tamest form, into the proverbial cold feet, or at its harshest, into full-blown conflict that starts you thinking about possible face-saving strategies for returning all those recently received engagement gifts. Finding yourself at odds with your future spouse when you feel you should be at your greatest unity is a very common and frightening experience. Fear not.

Throughout this book, you will begin to learn some ways of recognizing and managing what I have been describing, but for now, the best thing you can do is take that deep breath and begin to come to terms with the fact that for better or worse, although it is your wedding, it's not about you!

YOU CAN PAY (ATTENTION TO)
ME NOW OR YOU CAN PAY
THE LAWYER LATER

I am a gatekeeper. I admit it. It comes with the job. As a pastor, if a couple wants to get married in my church, they have to get past me first. Some people might call me a kind of religious bouncer who lets only the right people into the club, but the truth is that there are good reasons why almost all churches and other religious institutions have a requirement that those who wish to have a religious ceremony officiated by a member of their clergy (or in their building) must participate in some form of pre-marital preparation offered by, or approved of by, the religious institution. But if I am a gatekeeper, I am a poor one; I have only refused to perform one wedding for a couple that belonged to my church. If you had heard their story, you would have bounced them too. They were a statistic waiting to happen.

There are, of course, good religious reasons for this requirement. Faith traditions have great wisdom to offer couples. The idea of covenant is one of the most powerful. The great Biblical and ethical themes of faithfulness, compassion, forgiveness, justice, and, of course, love, are endless sources of strength and hope in relationships of all kinds, especially marriages. These we simply cannot ignore.

But beyond the religious reasons, the more practical reason is that compulsory pre-marital preparation is society's last and best hope to get a couple to spend at least a few minutes thinking about their marriage in the

4

midst of the countless hours they spend planning the wedding.

In my experience, once the question has been popped and answered (or the whole "contract" negotiated as seems to happen more and more often), critical thinking and long term planning go out the window in the rush of emotion generated by an engagement and the planning of a wedding. With the church reserved, the reception hall booked, and the invitations mailed, eyes glaze over at such mundane tasks as fleshing out what commitment and faithfulness really mean over the long term. Maybe you can see the problem forming.

Certainly, most couples have hopes and dreams for their long-term future together, but they don't generally have a plan for even the day following the honeymoon much less for years down the road. Many pre-marital preparation programs ask the useful question, "Where do you see yourselves five or ten years from today?" but pose it in the abstract. Even the most thoughtful couple will have trouble imagining more than where they will live, how many children they may have, or what their earning power may be.

A more useful form of that question would be, "What plans do you have in place over the next five or ten years for your individual emotional and spiritual growth, and for developing a healthy balance between self and couple?" I suspect that this question would stop most people in their tracks, and yet it may be the single most important question in preparing oneself honestly and thoroughly for the real challenges marriage presents a couple. But it is not a question you can answer on the spot.

And so now, before your wedding, you have a wonderful opportunity if you choose to take it: to spend an amount of time equal to the importance of the project. If the required three hours you spend in my office are all you invest, so be it. Chances are I'll see you in my office again in a few years discussing the end of your marriage rather than the beginning.

But if you prepare for marriage the way you prepare for a career, or for running a marathon, or building a house or for anything else worth doing, I'll see you in my office again when I introduce you as mentors to another young couple that has also decided to take with utmost seriousness their preparation for the blessing of a life-long marriage.

As a pastor, I talk to more couples planning to get married than most people, and I can confirm that most of them have their heads in the clouds. And so it occurred to me that perhaps the time to address the issues we normally cover in pre-marital preparation is not after there is an engagement ring on the bride's finger, but when that first surprising and thrilling, but unsettling, notion arrives on the scene that maybe this is "the One." I suppose you could call it pre-engagement preparation.

And so, lately I've been talking more to people who are not yet blinded by the planning stage, but who are in the "thinking about it" stage, people who are in mid- to long-term relationships that have not yet formalized into engagements. And I have been asking them what they would like to get out of pre-marital preparation when that time comes. What do they think they need to know to be able to stay married "till death do we part"?

For the most part, their answers (and maybe especially their non-answers) have been helpful and confirm that what I offer in this book is a helpful addition to the excellent resources already available. But one recent response in particular reminded me what is at stake for not investing at this stage of the game. In a joking way, but with a serious edge, one young man said to me, "I want to know what it will cost me to get a divorce."

"That's interesting," I replied, "because I have always said that you can pay me now, or you can pay the lawyer later – and I'm a lot cheaper." He just smiled.

The next four chapters make the case for why it is worth the time to not only read this book, but to actually begin to practice what it preaches.

Keep reading.

UNPACK BEFORE YOU MOVE IN

These are the things you should pay attention to in other books on preparation for marriage:

- How to manage your finances together
- How to avoid emotional and/or sexual infidelity
- How to fight fair
- How to understand the opposite gender
- How to raise children
- How to practice your faith together
- How to relate sexually
- How to communicate effectively
- How to be a man or woman of good character

These are all topics worthy of your study, conversation, and practice, offered by professionals in the field with years of experience. You will be well served by them.

Unfortunately, you can be an expert on each and every one of them, and still end up divorced or married "unhappily ever after."

That is because the one thing that can make all of those efforts truly effective is absent from virtually every other resource available to brides- and grooms-to-be, namely, the perspective contained in this book.

I know it sounds pompous for me to say I have the "one ring to rule them all," but it's true, or at least it has been in my own life and in the lives of couples with whom I have worked. Please hear me out.

What you will read in these pages is derived from a way of viewing the world called "Family Systems" thinking, a method first elaborated by thoughtful psychiatrists in the 1950s and continued by those, like myself, who have seen what a powerful tool it is to view and navigate life in family, workplace, religious institution, and civil society.

As you are each coming from a family, and beginning a new one, I believe there is no better way to leverage the wisdom of the experts in all the topics mentioned at the beginning of this chapter than by helping you to see the way your new family works in a systemic way.

Perhaps the most powerful tendency experienced by newly married couples is to see themselves as the center of the known universe, burning with a love so bright that it will illumine the darkest corners of creation. I know that is how I felt as my bride and I walked out of the church so many years ago. We were invincible!

And yet the power of that idea is also its greatest weakness because it doesn't take long to learn that there were a thousand other centers of the known universe forming on the same Saturday in August, and that nobody else thinks your love is as capable of transforming the universe as you do! And you quickly learn that you are still the same two people you were before you got married, only now the stakes are a lot higher.

And you suddenly began to feel a lot smaller and a lot more subject to the stresses that come with living under the same roof with a person who has not only moved his or her (choose one: tacky/girly) belongings into your new abode, but his or her emotional baggage as well. Believe me, that ugly lamp is the least of your problems!

It is the unpacking of these emotional suitcases that you are preparing for now, before the wedding. I know of no better way to organize the stuff that comes out of them than by understanding them as part of a complex, multi-generational, sometimes highly anxious system, of which you, individually and together, are both small and key parts.

(Incidentally, if you are already living together and thinking that you've already got this part covered, that you've finished your unpacking, I have news for you. It doesn't matter if you have lived together for years...it WILL be different once you actually get married. I guarantee it!)

I have learned all of this the hard way, through trials in my own marriage, through conflict on the job, by seeing how hard we struggle as a society to live up to the opportunity our civic unity offers us, and by working with couples who come to me in crisis, as they feel their bright star losing its intensity.

I offer this humbly, but with great confidence. I have used this method for years in preparing couples to be married, and I can happily report that my "batting average" makes me a good candidate for the Premarital Counseling Hall of Fame.

What's Love Got to Do With It?

These will be my only words about the popular topic of love: *it is not enough.* You have probably heard that before. It is both good and common wisdom. The formula for exactly what is enough varies from relationship to relationship, but the usual extra ingredients are some combination of faith, trust, commitment, and perseverance.

There is an old country music song by the group Girls Next Door that proclaims that "Love will get you through times with no money better than money will get you through times with no love" and it speaks the truth. However, when there is no money, if all you have is love, you will argue and fight a lot more. You can count on it.

Perhaps removing love from the recipe might not be a bad idea since all it does is cloud our judgment. I think Tina Turner asked the right questions a long time ago when she sang, "What's love got to do with it? What's love but a second-hand emotion?"

That song, "What's Love Got to Do With It?," is about two lovers, one of whom has crossed that delicate line in a relationship, and has declared true love for the other. And Tina's response, in so many words, is this: "Don't go spoiling a good thing by gettin' all mushy on me. I don't have time or energy for romance and sentimentalism. I'm just in this thing to have a good time and if you bring that baggage on up in here with you, it's only going to wreck a good thing."

Well, as jaded and as cynical as that might be, Ms. Turner's rejection of her lover's affections is perhaps a good and honest reminder for us not to let our love become too clouded by emotion, lest we ruin a good thing.

Of course, I am speaking about love in the sense it is perceived in that most romantic phase of our relationships, the feeling that is so often responsible for the question, "Will you marry me?", that has led you to this book.

No, love is not enough. Unless it is the right kind.

I am proposing that the love you need is what you could call "disinterested" love. That doesn't sound very appealing, I know, but bear with me for a moment while I contrast "disinterested" with its cousins "self-interested" and "uninterested".

Self-interested Love sounds intriguing until we see that it is always seeking something for itself. It is that realm of flirting, infatuation, and obsession, even stalking. It burns white hot and then burns out. It is the "I can't live without you, baby" material of rock songs that so easily degenerates into the dismissive "you were interesting to me as long as nothing else more interesting came along." Maybe you've been there. It hurts.

On the other hand, *Uninterested Love* is a cold, hard reality faced by too many couples. It conjures images of an old, stoic Norwegian couple sitting in rocking chairs by the fireplace someplace in Minnesota, nodding rather than speaking. There may be mutual support and admiration, but each is more content to co-exist than to risk inter-acting authentically. Masquerading as commitment, it's saying, "I am as uninterested in investing myself in you as I am divorcing you, because either way, it would just be too complicated." You don't want to end up here. It hurts.

Not surprisingly, *Disinterested Love* is neither of these. It is the love proclaimed by our faith traditions, the one that faces reality about the day-to-day ups and downs we experience in our emotions. What makes a person "disinterested" is that his or her perception of how "in love" they feel is not the basis on which to evaluate the health of their relationship, or the behavior within it. Disinterested lovers are equally concerned with what happens outside the relationship and within it. Disinterested lovers worry less about the emotional state of the relationship than their own emotional state. Disinterested lovers can make these kinds of statements (and mean them!):

- "I would hate to live without you, but I can do it."
- "I will do whatever it takes to make myself the best person I can be, with or without you."
- "You make me happy, but my happiness does not depend on you. And I will do everything I can to make you happy but I cannot accept the responsibility for your happiness."

Disinterested Love is the hardest kind, but the good news is that if you work on being *disinterested* in one another, romance will take care of itself. If this doesn't make perfect sense now, don't worry. I'm still figuring it out too. But the rest of the book fleshes out what it means to love disinterestedly and I think in the end you will see why the answer to "What's love got to do with it?" is both everything and nothing at all.

FOR THOSE WHO ARE RELIGIOUS

You may be wondering why a book on an institution as near and dear to religion's heart as marriage, written by a pastor, is addressing the role of faith and the Bible only now, and then only sparingly thereafter.

It is not, of course, because I think that Scripture, Church tradition, and personal faith have nothing to speak to couples preparing to get married. It is just that when they do, couples usually fall asleep! I tried that approach once upon a time.

My own experience with pre-marital preparation was offered in the pastor's office and for as much as I liked and admired the fellow who sat and talked with us, I can't for the life of me remember a word of what he said, especially about religious matters, except that he likened marriage to the Biblical concept of covenant, which, although powerful and true, has really only mattered to me later as a pastor, and not so much as a husband.

In fact, that experience of pre-marital counseling was so uninspiring that my bride-to-be and I went in search of it from another source, which spent almost no time on the matter from a faith perspective, and about which I remember much more, and even still refer to its printed materials from time to time. Not that it was perfect, but it was certainly a lot more engaging, and, over time, useful.

This is to say that when we find ourselves trying to manage our relationship in the midst of arguing with our spouses about whose turn it is to get up and tend to a crying child in the middle of the night, or when we slam the door after an argument about sex, or when our in-laws arrive unannounced and say they are staying for a week, theological insights and memorized Bible verses are not the tools that will get the job done. (In fact, these are used more often as weapons than tools. I have had more than my share of spouses asking me to use specific passages of the Bible – the ones that support their position in a conflict – to get their spouse in line.)

The other reason religious matters are of marginal usefulness at this stage of your preparation to be married is that there is little evidence that either faith or church attendance matter in the divorce statistics (or the count of the unhappily married). In fact, the most accurate thing you can say is that married couples are more likely to attend church than single people, a fact I chalk up more to them wanting to have their children in Sunday School.

Please do not misunderstand me. I strongly believe that faith and religious practice, Scripture, and maybe most of all, community, are indispensable to a healthy, stable, and fulfilling marriage. Ignore them at your peril! But we also cannot think they are some kind of force field around marriages that will protect them from heartbreak, an unspoken but powerful belief many couples hold about church weddings.

So here is where I see faith and religion, and particularly the Bible, being useful to the project of your preparation for marriage: that in the stories of our ancestors of the faith, and in our faith communities when they are honestly and faithfully seeking to live out the truths of those stories, we find the strength and hope to persevere in both our marriages and in our own formation as better husbands or wives. In our traditions of prayer and generosity we find ways to open ourselves to seek change not in our spouses but in ourselves. When we share ourselves with others in intentional ways in a faith community, we find opportunities to love and serve that put both our sometimes petty grievances and our greater conflicts with our spouse into perspective.

But let me conclude this chapter by more specifically addressing the role of the Bible in this book, and in your marriage. What I think you will find in reading both the Jewish and Christian Scriptures is God leading us to health and wholeness by living in the creative tension between "I" and "we," between "I" and "Thou," and between the past, the present, and the future. Each of these points of tension is lived in the systems we inhabit as married people who remain the children of others, and who become the parents of the next generation. Especially in the stories of Jesus, but also the older prophets, we find him embodying the characteristics of healthy relationships you will find throughout this book. You will find no better guide.

As confusing as it often is even for the most ardent theologians, the doctrine of the Holy Trinity is a brilliant illustration of the divine balance between self and other which will be the focus of this book. Each "person" of the Trinity is unique, with specific roles and characteristics, and yet is in the kind of perfect communion and harmony with the others that we desire with our spouses (and hopefully all of our other relationships!).

My prayer for you as you read this book is that you find your self, your marriage, and your faith strengthened.

HOW TO USE THIS BOOK

With these preliminary thoughts behind us, you are almost ready to dive into the heart of the matter. Before you do, let me share these final words about how to make the best use of this book.

As will be made clear in the very next chapter, the material you will read will not address the traditional themes in pre-marital preparation, at least not directly.

Instead, it invites you into a process of continual self-reflection about who each of you are as individuals, and also together as a couple, and how you will manage your emotional life in the context of the stresses and strains which will inevitably come your way.

That said, this book will describe in general terms the dynamics of what you are likely to face, especially early on in your marriage, offer you a new perspective on how to view them, and provide a few insights about how you can begin to manage them.

The five parts of the book follow a logical order in understanding your new life together. Each part is divided into five short chapters that are designed to give you just enough to begin a conversation, but not so much you will feel overwhelmed. You may find (as I often have) that you will be left wanting, that you need to know more. Indeed, I hope that will be your experience and that it will provoke you to delve deeper in the years to come.

But for now, it is more important that you spend even some time with this material, and I know how daunting a long and complex book can be. So, I will keep it short, and hope you take advantage.

At the end of each chapter are three questions designed to involve you in the conversation, at an individual level and with your partner. These are not test questions; there are no right or wrong answers. They are invitations you would be wise to accept.

There is also a suggested exercise for you to do which offers you a safe and interesting means of drawing on the wisdom of others about what you are reading here.

Here are a couple proposals for how to read this book, each with its own advantages and disadvantages. One way would be for each partner to read a chapter on their own, spend some time with the questions, and then come together for a time of sharing thoughts and insights generated by the readings.

Another option would be for you to read the book out loud together, taking turns reading chapters, or portions of chapters, and then discuss the questions directly and immediately. This method offers more spontaneous, and less guarded, reactions and responses.

Either way, the book is constructed in a way such that it can be read easily and thoughtfully over the course of five weeks. I might suggest reading the introduction to each part on the first day of your week, then one chapter a day during the week, leaving the final day for rest.

But no matter how you choose to read it, hold it lightly. It does not have answers for all your questions, but it will lead you to them eventually.

And now a word about what to do with it when you finish it. On one hand, I would be flattered if when you complete this book, you passed it on to another recently engaged friend (or better yet, someone thinking about getting engaged!) because you couldn't wait to share what you'd learned with someone else. A reader's delight is one of an author's greatest rewards.

On the other hand, I'll probably be even more gratified if you hold on to it for when you will need it again, because usefulness may be an even greater reward than delight. That is because if you hold on to this book, and even let it gather a little dust, it means that you both found something valuable in it, and also recognize that you will need it again in the future. Because you will. Nobody gets this stuff right the first time. I return time and time again to the resources that helped form the perspective I am sharing with you because they are a bottomless well. I hope this book will be that for you too.

It may be that you keep it just to look back at your answers on your fifth or tenth or twentieth wedding anniversary. That would be fine too. I could live with that.

Part Two

You are Not Marrying Your Fiancé/Fiancée – You are Marrying His or Her Family

You have heard, of course, of "The Big Three" — the three most commonly cited reasons for divorce:

- Money
- Sex
- In-laws

Perhaps these three top the list because they are the three indisputably present factors in a every couple's life. You need money to survive. If regular sex isn't considered an obligation, it is certainly at least one person's expectation. And everyone brings to a marriage a family of some kind, even if it is the nuns who raised you at the orphanage (more on the nuns later).

What I hinted at in the last chapter I want to make perfectly clear here, that your families of origin *will* make their presence felt in your marriage one way or another. What I want to do in this part is help you make it a wonderful and affirming presence rather than a torturous one. You see, the ugly fact about those stereotypically evil mothers-in-law is that they don't rise up out of the shadowy depths of hell all on their own. They are actually co-created by unwitting sons-in-law and daughters-in-law who somehow were lured into the mistaken belief that their marriage was their own domain.

Yes, the inescapable fact of your new marriage is that you will need to learn how to (at the very least) co-exist not only with your spouse, but with his or her family too (and some of your own as well, now that things are different). That is because you did not really marry just your spouse. You married his or her whole family, for the same better or worse, and 'till death do you part (and actually even after that too; again, more on that soon).

This is an old truism, of course, but one easily forgotten as the champagne glasses rise in celebration of an engagement. Before the toast "To the new couple!" is even finished, diplomatic strategies and battle plans are already unconsciously forming. A political realignment is coming to both of your families. No one will be left unscathed.

If that all sounds pretty conspiratorial, it's all in good fun. However, it really does describe what is happening. Two great clans are integrating whether they know it or not, and whether they like it or not. And you are the centerpiece of the deal. It is not exactly mergers and acquisitions, but it comes close. And they will be bound together forever – so they had better learn to like (or at least politely tolerate) each other so you can spend more time worrying about money and sex.

What this means for you now as you prepare for your marriage is that the better you understand how each of your families work (and also how families function in general), the better equipped you will be to head off the creation of the proverbial mother-in-law from hell for which you would be partly responsible.

This is not to charge you alone with the responsibility for harmonious relationships with your spouse's family, but to make sure you are aware of your role in them. Just because you are younger and newly married does not grant you automatic victim status any more than your respective mothers-in-law can claim it because they did not have any say in the choice of their new son-in-law or daughter-in-law (like in the good old days). You may never be able to arrive at a positive relationship with your in-laws, but that can't be for your lack of trying. I'm picking on mothers-in-law but of course this applies to anyone in your families.

And while the new in-laws get all the (bad) press, the reality is also that once you get married, relationships with members of your own family change. As much as it is a celebration, marriage involves a certain sense of grief and loss for the newlyweds and for their parents and others. There is a reason why the pastor keeps some Kleenex in the pocket of his or her robe at the wedding ceremony.

In some cases, you may literally be leaving your childhood home to move into your new family's dwelling, and that will require a period of adjustment. But even if you have lived on your own for years, your new status will provoke changes in your relationship with your own parents. I do not mean to suggest that these changes will lead to conflict, simply that if you fail to factor them in, you are far more likely to be caught emotionally flat-footed when you or someone else bumps into them, and miss the opportunity to make this transition a more graceful one.

I hope it goes without saying that I know I am employing a common stereotype about the nature of the relationship between newlyweds and their in-laws and that there are countless stories of powerfully nurturing and caring relationships forged by marriage. I know of many, many cases in which a strong relationship has remained with the in-laws even after the dissolution of a marriage, stronger with the ex- than with their own child.

But to ignore the prevalence of this kind of conflict and the effect it has on marriages is irresponsible, and so I invite you to take the time to examine your role in the relationships that are already developing, and to plan wisely for how you will do your part to keep the world safe from yet one more rampaging mother-in-law.

As you will see, what is important about understanding how your families work is not only how to head off conflict with in-laws, but even more importantly how to pave the way for each of you to relate more effectively with the other about every other aspect of your life together. Knowing more about the common emotional practices of families, how anxiety affects a family, and how families react or respond to that anxiety will give you a better chance at avoiding "The Big Three" or indeed any other reason that might keep you from enjoying the fulfilling marriage you deserve.

HOW BIG IS YOUR BEAKER?

There is a true story in my family that may or not be factually correct. Your families have these too.

My maternal grandparents owned and operated a drug store in San Antonio, Texas. My grandfather was the pharmacist and my grandmother tended the front end (with some help from my mother), including the soda fountain. Apparently, he was a good pharmacist, and the story begins when he was set to graduate from pharmacy school. All that remained was his final laboratory exam, the kind in which you mixed up a remedy of some kind under the watchful eye of the professor.

He went into the lab along with another student and they were given the recipe to prepare. Each was given the same instruments, measuring equipment, and chemical elements. The moment of truth arrived and my grandfather pulled out a large beaker, while the other student pulled out a much smaller beaker. And just as my grandfather was about to begin mixing his ingredients, the professor pulled him aside and took him out of the lab.

My grandfather was dismayed, certain he had failed the test, but the professor assured him that in fact not only had he passed, but that he needn't even finish it. You see, the professor knew that my grandfather knew that upon mixing the two ingredients in that recipe the resulting chemical reaction would come flowing out of a beaker the size chosen by the other student. My grandfather's beaker was big enough.

Marriage is a mixture of volatile chemicals. Each of you brings the emotional properties and characteristics—the virtues and vices, the strengths and weaknesses, and both the annoying and endearing habits and idiosyncrasies—of your families to the laboratory, and there *will* be a reaction. The question you need to ask yourselves right now is whether your beaker is big enough.

The size of the reaction of the mixture of your familial properties doesn't really matter. It can be small or large. Some are just a small fizz while others are a mighty explosion. What really matters is that your beaker is big enough for the size of your reaction. The good news is that there is always a big enough beaker available, if you choose to make it big enough. And by making it big enough, I mean each of you working individually and as a couple to mature emotionally and stay cool under pressure.

It is a wonder more fistfights don't break out at weddings. Although it is a staple of Hollywood films, I've only seen one fight break out at a wedding. Actually, it was at the reception, on the dance floor, and it was mostly two drunk guys ineptly flailing away at each other surrounded by a lot of women screaming at them to stop, which they did, not because one was victorious, but because they were both so vain they didn't want to muss their suits.

It was never clear why these two guys came to blows, but it doesn't really matter. Their fight started like most marital fights; not because there was a good reason, but because there was someone there to fight with! Under normal circumstances, bumping into someone on the dance floor doesn't provoke a fight. But weddings are not normal circumstances. They are often seething cauldrons of anxiety with a veneer of celebration.

What will cause most of your marital discord is that you will "bump into one another" at those moments when you are less able to manage your emotions, when you are not able to recognize your dance floor collision as simply being at the same place at the same time while both of you are having fun dancing to whatever beat or style pleases each of you. For example, under ideal circumstances, your spouse arriving late to meet you for an appointment is an opportunity for you to read another chapter in that book you are enjoying. But when you are stressed (consciously or unconsciously) that same late arrival is just the excuse you needed to criticize or blame, and the next thing you know, your mutual overreaction has overflowed onto the floor and it will take a lot of effort to clean it up.

What is important to recognize is that your ability to manage your emotions—to change the size of your beaker—is not about changing who you are. It is about controlling the environment in which the inevitable reaction takes place. You cannot change the properties of the chemical you bring to the mix any more than salt can stop being the exact combination of sodium and chloride that makes it salt. But you can control the circumstances in which your salt and your spouse's vinegar mix.

Helping you do that is the task of later chapters in this book. For now, let's work on helping you understand your "chemical" makeups, and what causes you to fizz or explode together.

QUESTIONS

What do you think are some of your family's "chemical properties"?

How have you seen these family properties interact with the properties of other families?

How big a beaker do you think you will need? Do you feel equipped to alter the size of that beaker as needed?

* * *

EXERCISE

Seek some stories among your family members that speak some truth (even if they aren't necessarily factual) about your family. Perhaps write them down and tuck them in the back of this book for later review.

YOU CAN RUN BUT YOU CAN'T HIDE

You do not exist. Let me explain. Biologically speaking, you probably understand that you only exist as a result of your parents coming together in that certain, special way.

But since you were born, you have had instilled in you a very powerful sense of identity, your own unique identity, as unique as a snowflake or a fingerprint. This is a very common way of viewing the world from a Western point of view, Descartes's "I think, therefore I am," and all of that. You generally think and feel from an "I" point of view. I love, I feel, I go to work, and so on. Yes, you are truly one of a kind.

From this systems point of view that I am sharing with you, however, "I"s don't really exist. You are not only biologically a product of your parents, hardwired with their DNA, but even more importantly, you are the inheritors of your family's "emotional DNA". You have been inescapably conditioned by your family's story – its myths, its surroundings, its stresses, its victories, its losses, its saints, its secrets, its love and its lies. It doesn't matter if they really happened. What matters is that the family believes these things about itself and lives and acts accordingly. Incidentally, this is why it doesn't matter who raised you, whether a traditional pair, or grandparents, foster parents, nuns, or even wolves; you are still part of a family because you were involved in some configuration of relationships that passed on to you its collective emotional DNA, its way of relating to one another.

29

Let me tell you another "true" story from my mother's side of the family. We have relatives buried in Roselawn Cemetery in San Antonio, a lovely place with interesting headstones that contain a lot of history. One year, this cemetery was sold to a company that decided it would keep its profits up by keeping its maintenance costs down and so they opted for a new kind of lawnmower. To make this change possible, they contacted all the families for whom they had records to seek permission to change the positions of some of the headstones so that their more efficient equipment could pass through more easily. All of the plot owners agreed to this change, except one: my grandmother, who refused to allow the headstone of my grandfather to be turned the requested ninety degrees. And so to this day, his (and now hers) is the only headstone pointed in the opposite direction from all the rest.

Why is this important? As my wife will be happy to tell you, I began being a little more than ninety degrees off-axis long before I ever heard this story! It was not hearing the Roselawn story, per se, that made me the way I am. But my family's "story," which shaped my Grandmother's contrarian spirit, shaped mine too with this kind of family resemblance.

All of this is to say that I hear from many couples that they are sure they will not repeat their families' patterns or make the same mistakes, because they are their own people, in a new, independent entity. And they are not wrong. It is very possible to change patterns, and make different choices. But what I think they mean to say is that they will do this as if they did not come from the families from which they came! Digging a little deeper into the past, what they are likely to find is that it has long been a part of their families' stories to buck the system, to shake things up a little, and that they are not really the pioneers of that spirit, but rather the latest in a long line of people to carry on that particular form of family tradition.

I also encounter couples that decide to leave all the family drama behind and head out on a new trail on their own. They elope, or do not invite their families to the wedding or tell them they have married. They often go on to live their lives disconnected from those people from their pasts whom they feel are problematic or toxic. This is often a wise course of action; continuing in a relationship with an abusive family member does not lead to abundant life. But for that distance to really make more than a geographic difference in their lives, they must also deal with the emotional reality that whether or not they want to belong to their family of origin, they always will. This is hard, hard work.

At the risk of sounding overly dramatic, it is here that I want to urge both of you to be brutally honest about the state of your relationships outside your partnership. You can run from your past, but you cannot hide from it forever. Whatever you leave unresolved before the wedding will still be unresolved when you say, "I do." Your new family will not save you from your old one. Your marriage is not an escape pod. If either of you have relationships to repair, or trauma to reconcile, go and do it now (or at least get started), before it gets even more complicated later. And know that your decision about whether or not to do this will impact not only you, but your spouse and your children as well.

QUESTIONS

What emotional "family resemblance" do you see in your own family? In your future spouse's family? For example, carefree, worried, responsible, generous, etc.

What are the strengths of your family's way of relating to each other? Its weaknesses?

What relationships in your life need attention? What resources or support would you need to address these?

* * *

EXERCISE

Investigate your family's genealogy if you have not already done so. Check with other family members to see if anyone has already done it so you don't reinvent the wheel. If they have, see how you might further its work.

THE INHERITANCE THAT REALLY MATTERS

You are climbing the first hill on your very first roller coaster ride. All you can see are the tracks above you and the blue sky beyond. Your heart beats twice as fast as the clicks and clacks of the rickety car making its way to the top, slowly but surely. You remember the screams of others before you. The suspense is agonizing, unbearable even. You hope it will last, that rush of adrenaline.

I hope you are feeling that pleasant form of anxiety in these weeks and months leading up to your wedding. You probably felt it in that moment when one of you proposed and the other accepted. You will feel it many times throughout your marriage. When it happens, stop and give thanks.

There will be other times, however, when you want to curse the anxiety you are feeling, the not-so-pleasant kind that keeps you awake at night, that makes you irritable at your spouse or children, that makes you stay at the office an hour or two longer than you should. You may even be feeling this kind of anxiety while reading this book as I suggest how much work marriage takes. This is the anxiety we all hope to avoid, with some people making a fine, but futile (and painful) art of the attempt.

But that will be impossible, because besides the proverbial death and taxes, anxiety is the third person in the Unholy Trinity of the inevitables in life. But just as death and taxes also have their benefits, so too does anxiety, both the pleasant, roller coaster kind, and the unpleasant, dark night of the soul kind. (If you have not already experienced the latter, you'll just have to trust me for now.)

So you can expect anxiety to be a significant factor in your marriage, and in order to make the best use of it, it may be helpful to know more about it, where it comes from, where it is going, and how you can manage it.

Let me begin with a working definition: Anxiety is. It just is.

I suspect this will not be very satisfying, but the truth about anxiety is that it is present in all relationships, it is perfectly normal, and it manifests itself in everyone a little differently. But if you want a more complete definition, here is one I have pulled together over the years: Anxiety is a morally neutral emotional stimulus that comes from a real or perceived threat. As I have said, it is neither good nor evil; anxiety simply is...creative, painful, delicious, burdensome, and so much more.

Here is another way of looking at it. Anxiety is like the electrical current in your home that passes easily over the wires it encounters, and seeks ultimately the path of least resistance. This is why our homes have electrical outlets with that third, round hole. We have installed a grounding system, which, if something is wrong with one of our home's electrical circuits, directs that dangerous current directly into the earth, instead of through us. Human beings are very conductive, for electricity and for emotional anxiety. I hope you see where I am headed.

I like this image of anxiety because it also corresponds to language we commonly use that speaks of how our brains, or our personalities, or our families are "wired." Indeed, I earlier referred to how your family's emotional processes are hardwired like emotional DNA. In many respects, the success of your marriage will depend on how well grounded it is, how well it directs its energy to where it is supposed to go.

Once you return from your honeymoon (but no later than when you have children), you should prepare your legal last will and testament. This document will direct the executors of your estate on how to distribute the inheritance your spouse or children will receive according to your wishes. Your survivors will thank you.

But for right now, you should be reviewing the emotional inheritance you have already received from your families, recognizing that their anxiety is the largest part of the estate. Along with all the other physical characteristics you have inherited, you have also received the sum total of generations' worth of anxiety, some of it directed into the earth where it belongs, but some of it still floating around waiting to shock you (in both creative and harmful ways, of course) if you touch an exposed wire (read: nerve).

And once you have seen where there might be some loose connections, frayed insulation, or just a really poorly installed circuit, you can go about and do your part to improve that wiring for your own comfort and safety, and that of the next generation. That is where we go from here in the next chapters: what to look for and some tips on how to get that system properly grounded.

QUESTIONS

What are some experiences of both the more pleasant and not-so-pleasant forms of anxiety you have experienced?

How do you perceive your family's ability to deal with anxiety? What are the effects of their successes or failures?

What emotional inheritance would you like to pass on to your children? Try to go a little deeper than "love."

* * *

EXERCISE

Search for quotes on anxiety to get a better sense of the way it has been experienced through the ages.

My Enemy is Your Enemy

Even before we were married, my wife and I touched a live wire, and got shocked. I ran afoul of one of her family's unwritten rules, and neither of us knew how to deal with it.

At that time, we lived in different cities, several hours apart, and I would make frequent trips to visit her. On one trip, we spent a lovely afternoon at the home of a friend of her family. I quite liked this friend of theirs and looked forward to seeing him again on my next visit.

It was not to be. When I arrived on my next trip, I suggested we visit him and my then-fiancée told me that would not be possible. Naturally, I inquired whether he had moved or died, but she said no. And so I pushed, and tensions rose, and finally she revealed that although she too would have liked to visit him, her mother had had a falling out with the guy and therefore we would not be able to go. And I thought that was the most ridiculous thing I had ever heard. What did her mother have to do with a simple visit to a friend? Who cares? So I announced that I would just go by myself, and then the battle was really joined. Purple hearts were awarded that day.

What I later was able to understand was that one of her family's unwritten rules (at least in those days) was that "My enemy is your enemy," and that I was asking her, in a very real sense, to betray her family. An unwritten rule is one of a family's ways of defining itself, of setting its boundaries. If you follow the rules, you are one of us. If you don't, there will be consequences: you may get to stay in the family, but we will act differently toward you until you come around. Unwritten rules are normal and often useful. They can also be very complex and constraining.

These family rules, written and unwritten (which is to say conscious and unconscious), exist to help a family maintain its emotional equilibrium, its sense of balance. If you have ever watched a mobile hanging over a baby's crib, you have a good sense of a system's equilibrium. If you touch even one dangling piece, every other piece moves, some of them even more forcefully than the initial movement. Due to their radical interconnectedness, families are keenly aware when one of their members is moving or changing. And this is one of those morally neutral emotional stimuli we call anxiety.

The current level of a family's anxiety can often be measured by how strictly it polices its rules. In families where overall anxiety is lower, there is more flexibility around the edges. You can get away with certain infractions while the cops are at the donut shop. But in more highly anxious families, it is difficult to avoid being caught in the glare of flashlights in the dark when you are trying to sneak around where you are not supposed to be.

The bigger issue with these rules is that when you get married, you begin to make regular incursions across the border with another country. You spend more time relating with your in-laws, you begin to let down your guard, you start smuggling in new and exotic trinkets and spices from foreign lands, and then it happens: Zappf! Like a spy deemed a threat to national security, you wind up in prison a long way from home without a clue about how the legal system works.

As in my case, you are usually busted right at the border, by the front line. Normally, your spouse will serve as the border agent, enforcing the rules on behalf of the state. You never even get a sideways glance from the higher-ups because they have been kept in the dark. It is dealt with at the lowest levels. But if you insist on appealing to the Emperor, and bring the matter to the attention of the whole of your spouse's family, you run the risk of sparking a larger battle in which both you and your spouse will find yourselves in the crossfire.

What makes all this so challenging is that running afoul of one of your spouse's family's unwritten rules puts your spouse in a virtual, and anxiety-producing, no-win situation. He or she will enter into some level of conflict with either you or his or her family, and anxiety will probably rise in all parties. This is why it is important to bring to the surface now the unwritten rules that unwittingly guide your behavior, as well as to learn how to deal with border disputes when they arise. This way, no one feels squeezed to that point of a defensiveness that invites an even greater counter-reaction.

As I said, it took me a long time (years, really) to understand what had happened. But it took even longer to see that my reaction to my wife's closing of the border was partly because in the ensuing discussion, she had just as unwittingly violated one or more of my family's unwritten rules, like "Thou shalt not tell me who my friends can be" or "The one with the last word wins." I did not know how to let it be, and she did not know how to stand up to her family and risk the consequences. Both of us were the poorer for both the argument and the loss of a friend. Neither was necessary, but neither of us knew how to manage the anxiety that the situation engendered. Feel free to learn from our mistakes.

QUESTIONS

What are some of your family's rules, both written and unwritten?

When members of your family have challenged those rules, what has been the response?

How do you think my wife and I could have handled the situation differently, to still be able to meet our friend? Or choose a similar example from your own relationship and discuss how it could have gone differently.

* * *

EXERCISE

Watch the movie, "The Family Stone." See if you can identify some of the characteristics of families that I have been suggesting.

TRIANGLES ARE THE NEW CIRCLES

When my then-fiancée and I visited my grandmother for the first time after announcing our engagement, she presented us with a quilt she had begun making while she was pregnant with my father and then had finished a few years later. I don't know much about quilt designs, but I'm told that it is the double wedding ring pattern, which you can see pretty clearly when it is spread out upon the bed on a beautiful summer day. It turns out that all the bits of colored fabric that make up the rings of the pattern are pieces of my grandmother's maternity dresses, quite a statement of family unity and tradition, and beautiful beyond belief.

If you have not already, you will spend some time searching for the perfect wedding ring, a powerful symbol of love and commitment principally because of its shape. The shape of a circle evokes completeness, eternity, tranquility. There are no rough edges on a circle. As we felt when we first laid eyes on my grandmother's quilt, circles are the perfect geometric representation for the promise a wedding holds.

Circles are not so perfect, however, for the reality a marriage brings. That is because the shape that will more frequently impact your marriage is the triangle. Don't worry; I am not implying you will somehow become involved in a Hollywood-style "love triangle." Rather, you will become involved in the natural and normal emotional triangles that all families and relationships use as a primary means of dealing with the anxiety generated by

41

those "real or perceived" threats to their integrity, of enforcing those unwritten rules.

Maybe the simplest way to understand an emotional triangle is as an attempt to deal indirectly with an emotion we can't deal with directly. Since most of our emotions, especially stress, are experienced in a relationship with someone else, we are faced with the choice of dealing directly with that person, or choosing another option. Maybe you can see the triangle forming.

So, for example, when you seek advice from someone on how to deal with a difficult decision you must make, you are triangling. When your friend comes to hang out with you to cool down rather than punch someone out, a triangle has saved someone's face from punishment. Gaining perspective is one of the benign forms of triangulation.

Where triangles become more problematic is when they are used to avoid the interactions we really need to have, and become merely a means of blowing off steam. Then they lose their positive value and assume their negative value of simply transferring anxiety. Recalling our illustration of the electrical current, the third party in a triangle is viewed as the path of least resistance.

What happens when a triangle is successfully formed is that the person who has been triangled then receives a not-so-special gift of the anxiety that should be dealt with elsewhere. Frequently, that anxiety becomes a reason for conflict with the final person involved. Maybe you have had the common experience of having a friend come to you to complain about how a third person has mistreated your friend. Your anxiety rises in defense of the injustice and you may even be moved to confront the so-called aggressor head on. The result is that you end up with a new enemy while your friend feels oh-so-relieved at having an ally (even though you and the aggressor had nothing between you to begin with).

It may be helpful to know that the third "person" in a triangle is not always a person. It can be a behavior, a cause, a disease, anything that allows a person to (over)focus on something else less painful and avoid the hard, emotionally risky work of bringing anxiety to a proper resolution. Sometimes what even seem to be virtues mask our inability to address our anxiety, as with, for example, overachieving, or going out of our way to help other people.

The greatest tragedy of triangles is not only that they can bring into conflict two (or more) people who have no reason to fight. It is also that as long as the triangling goes on, the initial anxiety is never addressed. This means that the same unresolved emotion can be the source of an endless stream of conflicts with the wrong person, each appearing as if they were a new problem in their own right, and never allowing the real issues to surface.

The way I hope this will be useful information for you is so that you can begin to recognize those points in your life where your anxiety may incline you to triangle your spouse, or when you wonder why you are suddenly at odds with your spouse for no apparent reason. It is also to help you see that one of the best things you can do for your spouse, or any member of your families, is to refuse to be triangled and to help redirect appropriately that energy.

What too often happens is that our anxiety makes us try to beat a triangle back into being a circle. And that never works. We'll see why in the next part.

QUESTIONS

What are some of your experiences of being triangled? Of triangling others?

Where can you see triangles at work in your family? How do they involve you?

In your own life, how have you generally avoided dealing with emotionally sensitive issues?

* * *

EXERCISE

Go through a favorite novel or television show and see if you can recognize the triangles.

PART THREE

THE BETRAYAL OF TOGETHERNESS

There is a wonderful comfort in companionship, in togetherness. We are not made to be alone. We are made for one another. Although this is a significant religious insight, it is also easily enough derived simply by looking around and noting that, except for the stray hermit, not many people choose to be alone for lengthy periods of time. That is why solitary confinement in prison is such a harsh experience for those who have been "in the hole" and social ostracism is so devastating for those who get excluded.

Yes, we may relish being out on our own in the wilderness for a time, alone with our thoughts, away from people clamoring for our attention, but sooner or later those thoughts turn to home, whatever that sense of home may be. You may already be experiencing the so-called "nesting instinct" common to many couples which finds them deriving great satisfaction choosing the china and other home furnishings for their gift registry. (Free tip: choose things with a wide variation in price!) But that satisfaction is not based on the quality or charm of the items you are choosing, but rather that you are choosing them together.

Many forms of pre-marital preparation focus on your level of compatibility, whether or not you have enough in common, so to speak, to make it over the long haul, and if you have a lot of differences, how to bring them in line to become more compatible. But I think you already know you are compatible. You wouldn't be engaged if you weren't. You wouldn't enjoy spending so much time together if you weren't. And as we have already seen, your differences, whatever they may be, don't really matter. What matters is how you each will manage your own reactions to those differences.

So I will assume that you know you have found the right person to marry. And I will also assume that you have roughly equal levels of emotional maturity. Although many divorced people would beg to differ, few people marry someone with a widely differing level of maturity. For the reasons I will share in the next chapter, a partner's choice of someone whom they later "figure out" was "so immature" says a lot about their own level of maturity.

And so you are wonderfully together, on a great many levels. Given our theological and societal beliefs about marriage, you could even say you are "stuck together," in joy and in sorrow, in sickness and in health, and in every other way. It sounds great, doesn't it? You have found the perfect person to be stuck with for the rest of your life!

Wait, that doesn't sound quite right...

Because it's not quite right. You see, although your togetherness doesn't feel like any kind of problem right now, it is precisely where you will feel it when a problem does arise. When that old "morally neutral emotional stimulus that comes from a real or perceived threat" intrudes itself, and it inevitably will, the very first place you are likely to react to it is in your sense of togetherness. In your gut, you will begin to feel either too close to your partner, or not close enough, and that will become your problem. Yes, anxiety will help you become acquainted with the betrayal of togetherness.

Before I say more about the betrayal of togetherness, let me set the stage for understanding it better. Despite what I said earlier that there really is no such thing as "I," it is pretty obvious that you experience your life as an "I" who is relationship with others. This implies then a sense of your independence, but also your dependence, your sense of self and your sense of community. As a result, all of your relationships, including your marriage, are lived out in a tension between the forces of separateness and closeness, because you have needs for both of those things, unless you are that stray hermit.

This is pretty basic stuff, but as an example, think back to when you had friends over for a party, and they overstayed their welcome. You were overjoyed with their company at the beginning, but later were desperate for them to leave so you could do the laundry, study, or just sleep. Your life needs that kind of balance to keep you emotionally stable.

Where it all becomes tricky in your marriage is when one of your relationships gets stuck too close to one end of that spectrum between closeness and separateness. When you become emotionally fused with someone, or when you become emotionally cut off from them, either your sense of "I" or your sense of "we" feels threatened. And then you will react, and nine times out of ten it will be your spouse who meets the leading edge of your reaction, no matter why, or with whom, you may feel anxious. The betrayal has struck.

You will experience the betrayal of togetherness in one of its two forms. You will feel either that your togetherness with your spouse has been betrayed (that it is slipping away) or you will feel that your togetherness has betrayed your sense of self (that it is suffocating you). You will either feel like your spouse has smashed the china you carefully chose together, or you will feel like throwing it at him or her yourself.

Not that you will be thinking about it in this analytical way. You'll just be involved in an unpleasant spat with your spouse about whose turn it is to take out the trash. But it will feel like a greater crisis than it probably is, because it is striking right at the very heart of your relationship, the part you are most thrilled about right now: your sense of blessed togetherness.

But fear not. This is part of marriage. All couples experience it to some degree. It is unavoidable. But it is not insurmountable. That is what this book is for.

Before we move forward into a few chapters that will help you understand all of this better, let me pull a few earlier themes back into the conversation. I hope you are seeing that part of your ability to love disinterestedly, to adjust the size of your beaker, is recognizing that your sense of togetherness will need to be flexible. It cannot remain fixed. While this may sound distressing at first, you will find great liberation later in knowing that your marriage will not only survive, but rather thrive, precisely because it does not depend on your perception of your togetherness.

And if you were wondering if it is possible to triangle your own relationship, the answer is a resounding yes. In fact, it is probably the most common way a couple enters into conflict: by over focusing on the state of the relationship at the expense of dealing with the real sources of anxiety behind the great betrayal of togetherness.

Go Ahead – Blame the Institution

To begin our look at togetherness, here is a true story that also happens to be factually correct.

Very early in our marriage, maybe even the first week after we returned home from our honeymoon, we were in the supermarket, going up and down the aisles choosing together what would fill our new shelves in our new kitchen in our new apartment in our new town. It was all so new and fun.

And then we arrived at the jam and jelly aisle, and I reached for a jar of raspberry jam, and before I could even set it in the shopping cart, my new wife asked, "What are you doing? I don't like raspberry. Let's get strawberry." And I replied something like that I thought strawberry was boring and that raspberry would really be a better choice. And back and forth the conversation went, getting edgier and edgier, until we finally decided on grape, since it was becoming clear that neither of us was going to convince the other.

You must be thinking, "Wow. How utterly stupid," and you would be right. Because it never occurred to us, not even for a second, that we could actually buy two different kinds of jam. We simply had to agree on everything that went into that basket. It wasn't as if we could only afford one. We weren't rich, by any means, but neither were we poor, and we were certainly well-educated enough to calculate that those two different jars of jam would last as long as two jars of a jam we could compromise on, but never fully enjoy. For weeks, maybe months, our tastebuds were betrayed by our newlywed's need for togetherness.

Unfortunately, tastebuds are the least of anyone's problems, and newlyweds frequently find themselves tied up in knots when the number and intensity of these kinds of incidents mounts. This is because early on in our marriages, we experience a profound, often overwhelming, need for togetherness, in part because it is so new and intoxicating, but perhaps also to prove to ourselves and anyone who might be looking on that, indeed, we really are right for each other.

If, in a few months (or even already), you find yourselves caught in this trap, you have my permission to forgive yourselves, and blame the institution—of marriage. Here's why marriage, rather than each other, is your problem: it was never designed to carry the emotional weight we now put on its shoulders.

To go back to our supermarket illustration, it wasn't really that many years ago when the wife would simply buy the jam and the husband would eat whatever was set before him. Or the husband would instruct his wife as to what kind of jelly to purchase, and she would do so. I know that sounds quite gender-bound, and stereotypical, but in general, household roles were much more strictly defined, even if they also led to having only one kind of jam in the house. For that very reason, I don't think the old way worked very well either. But neither did it lead to the ridiculous kind of argument my wife and I had in the jam and jelly aisle. My point here is that as unhappy as tastebuds may have been fifty years ago, there was not the same emotional expectation that both husband and wife should have to agree on the flavor they used.

This kind of joint decision-making we face today about relatively mundane stuff is a pretty modern phenomenon. For most of human history, and still in parts of the world today, marriage was considered a functional household arrangement with some nice side benefits: regular sex, economic security, and an expanded circle of social or business contacts through your in-laws. Despite our romantic projections into the past, there is little evidence that, on a broad scale, people married for the reasons we often do now: *meaningful* sex, *emotional* security, or, to be honest, *love*. Generally, men and women led pretty separate lives, coming together for certain practical matters (like meals and making babies) but largely having their emotional and companionship needs met by extended family and gender-specific circles of relationships.

For better or worse, marriage these days carries the expectation that you and your spouse will be the primary emotional supports for one another, rather than the secondary ones they have been traditionally. This puts an extraordinary pressure on each of you to feel responsible for the emotional health and well-being of your spouse, a weight that few marriages can support for very long. Ours felt that strain upon our very first trip to the supermarket together; neither of us wanted to make the other unhappy by not agreeing.

So, blame the institution. It has set you up to fail in the dream of togetherness. But that doesn't mean it has to be a nightmare. It shouldn't stop you from experiencing the blessings of emotional support from your spouse that our more modern conception of marriage now offers us. It just has to be done in a way that allows each of you the possibility to share the load instead of bearing it alone.

QUESTIONS

What expectations of emotional support and companionship do you have of your future spouse?

What are your current sources of emotional strength and security? How do you think these relationships might change once you are married?

What examples in your own life do you have for a balanced emotional support system? An unbalanced one?

* * *

EXERCISE

Ask your parents whom they would have chosen to be your spouse if "arranged marriages" were the norm for your culture. If they say it is your fiancé/fiancée, ask them for their second choice. Then ponder this...

COMPLEMENTARY NEUROSES

Every married couple can share a story about how they met, why they fell in love, or when they knew they wanted to marry. I am sure you have your own. And I am also almost as sure that the ending of your story is some variation of the feeling, "We just fit together" like a hand in the perfect glove or Cinderella's foot in the glass slipper. It's like being in a comfortable sofa from which you never want to get up. And that has little to do with who is the better cook or car mechanic. It's about how you feel together.

Nevertheless, even if your relationship has come together for more emotional reasons than it might have in the past, there is still a strong functional aspect to it beyond who does what chore. I am talking about what emotional roles you play in each other's life, and how that gets worked out in your marriage. I have no doubt that you are mutually supportive emotionally, but I also have no doubt that it is much more complex, and much more complementary, than just that. There is more to your story than you are able to tell us.

One of the most compelling reasons I have heard for why we choose our mate is that he or she is "the person who most perfectly complements our own neuroses." Whoever coined that phrase must have had a hell of a marriage!

But it makes sense if you understand what neurosis really is. A working, if Wikipedia, definition of neurosis is that it is "a class of functional mental disorders involving distress but neither delusions nor hallucinations, whereby behavior is *not* outside socially acceptable norms."

(Emphasis mine.) In other words, basically, who you are. That is why the term has largely been removed from the vocabulary of the so-called helping professions – because everyone is neurotic! It doesn't really say much more than that you are a human being journeying through life with the baggage I am suggesting you unpack before you move in. At the same time, however, the term captures the sum total of all that low-level, socially acceptable craziness we inherit through our family's unwritten rules, their ways of relating to one another, and their efforts to relieve their anxiety. In other words, our collective neuroses give our lives a certain emotional shape. We all have a shape.

Now think about your particular shape floating around in that perfect circle that is supposed to be a marriage. You are not going to stop bouncing around in there until you find that perfectly complementary shape you will one day call your spouse. If one of you has corners and the other one curves, you are not going to find that perfect match. Corners fit with corners and curves fit with curves. Maybe the yin and yang image is coming to mind, but it could also be a set of interlocking blocks, or two strings all tangled up together. The point is that they fit together and fill up that circle. Your perfect match.

Now, the way most people describe the complementarity they feel is with statements like, "She is so practical while I am so spontaneous." But I think what you will find is that it goes much, much deeper than that. You see, what the shapes in your circle represent are the complementary emotional needs that each of you has brought to the relationship, and these are the real reason you came together. Leaders need followers, lightning needs a lightning rod, actors need audiences, and vice versa, but these are not the way people perceive themselves in the midst of a relationship, at least not initially, and so they describe themselves in more superficial terms. When I ask couples in my office why they are together, no one ever says, "Because I am a needy, dependent person, and she/he likes to take care of me."

In ways that may not be clear now, you and your future spouse are already playing your emotional roles to perfection. By itself this fact means little. It works perfectly for you right now, and may do so for the foreseeable future. But neither of you will stay the same throughout your whole lives. Your change and growth is as inevitable as your finding one another. Your parents will age and die. Your children will grow up and move out (hopefully!). These things can be expected and you may even be able to plan for how you will adapt to some of them.

But you will also encounter endless unexpected twists and turns in your life that will impact you just as profoundly. This means that the emotional needs you have now will change as well, and when only one of the players changes, this produces the anxiety that we have seen is a threat to our sense of balance and togetherness. The circle is no longer so comfy.

You will dance together at your wedding reception. Maybe you are already practicing the steps so you won't be so embarrassed when the moment comes. One of you is probably a better dancer than the other, and you should let that person lead. But know that one day, the other person will need or want to do a new kind of dance step entirely, one that the other has never seen before. And unless you can both figure out how to let the other one lead, you will both find yourselves with swollen toes or worse.

QUESTIONS

What are the roles you play in the different systems of which you are a part, e.g. work, couple, family of origin? Do you play the same role in all of them?

What new emotional dance steps can you imagine yourself learning in the future?

Who can give you honest insight on the roles you play in your relationships?

* * *

EXERCISE

Draw, paint, sculpt or otherwise make a visual representation of how you see your complementary shapes fitting together in your circle.

You Can't Step on My Toes If I Run Away— Oh, Yes, I Can!

Talking about swollen toes reminds me of that old playground game (perhaps more common among boys, I don't know, but girls must have had something similar) in which two or more of you would stand across from one another, and try to step of the toes of your opponent, without getting your own stepped on. This game of fancy footwork would go on for a little while until eventually one person would tire of the game and walk away.

Well, at least at my school, that was not the end of the game. The person left standing there would usually follow after the one who had removed himself from the game, and try to continue to step on his toes, which would then lead to a chase, and ultimately to the kind of scuffle that would earn you the right to stay indoors during tomorrow's recess.

You see, unless it is by mutual agreement, stopping in the middle of the game is an act of bad sportsmanship, if not outright treason. It doesn't matter if it is baseball or hopscotch. You are supposed to be in the game, win or lose, until the end. That is one of the most important of a playground's unwritten rules.

This is an especially useful rule if you are very good at a certain game, because it keeps others in the game when they might have bailed out earlier, because let's face it, playing a game in which you have no chance of winning isn't very fun, and winners need losers. But it is also useful if you frequently have no one to play with, because once you are in the game, then it forces others to play with you longer then they normally would.

The title of Robert Fulghum's popular book, "All I Really Need to Know I Learned in Kindergarten," also applies to marriage. The togetherness and belonging games you played back then will be the same ones you play in your marriage. The main difference is that now you will end up with bruised egos instead of swollen toes.

Here's how it works. When you begin feeling that sense of the betrayal of togetherness I described earlier, whether it comes as feeling too close or too far away from your partner (too fused or too cut off), your instinctual need to restore your emotional equilibrium will kick in and provoke you to make a balancing move away from, or closer to, your partner. You will likely be completely unaware that you are doing this, but your partner will react, because his or her sense of emotional stability has also been upended. It is like stopping that playground game in the middle without agreeing to end it first.

Let me be clear here that this betrayal of togetherness is not caused by either partner. Remember, you are a perfect match! In fact it is very likely that the anxiety which provokes your need to change the emotional distance between you comes as a result of your connectedness and balance with other people in your larger system. Your spouse is not the only one with whom you have a contract of togetherness.

So, for example, say one of your mothers begins to react to the emotional distance created by your marriage, and becomes a more intrusive presence in her child's life, because, naturally, she misses her baby. One of the ways you might respond to this distance-reducing move of hers is by making one of your own toward your spouse. You want to spend more time with your spouse so you can spend less time with your suddenly clingy mother. And then she will respond by pursuing you even more, at the very same time your spouse is trying to move away from you (to reestablish the pre-invasion balance), and the next thing you know, everyone is cross with everyone else for reasons they can't understand.

Let me also be clear that the whole flow can move in the other direction. It could be you who feel grieved by the greater emotional distance from your mother, and make a move toward her that feels to your spouse like a move away from him or her. Like I said earlier, you can unwittingly help create the mother-in-law from hell.

I am describing this process of emotional movement because although it is completely ordinary, it is not obvious to most couples, and they are often blindsided by it. They simply feel abandoned or suffocated, and react accordingly. The other person, or the relationship itself, gets labeled as the problem, and off they go into a conflict that could have been avoided.

In the next chapter, I will be more specific about the forms this game-playing takes, but for now I want to make sure you have a chance to see what is happening to your togetherness on the unconscious level. With a little more understanding of your playground's emotional dynamics, you can avoid missing tomorrow's recess and keep on having fun together.

QUESTIONS

What was your actual childhood playground experience? Did you play well with others? Were you a loner?

How sensitive do you feel you are to the changes in other people's lives?

When faced with an anxiety-producing situation, are you more of a conflict avoider or a "stay and fight" kind of person?

* * *

EXERCISE

Go and watch children playing on a playground. Pay attention to their patterns of behavior, how their parents are involved (or not involved). What can you learn about yourself? Your family? Your partnership?

Stop Picking on Me!

A two-legged stool is inherently unstable. If you can even get it to stand up by itself, the slightest movement of the floor, someone sitting on it, or even a breath of wind will knock it over. This is why you rarely see two-legged stools. It is also why you rarely see couples without any conflict or emotional game-playing. This may sound rather sad and discouraging at first, but hold on for the happy ending.

As pathetic as it may sound, conflict and game-playing stabilize a couple and keep them from falling over (and apart). Look at it this way, given the option between falling over and not falling over, which do you choose? It is not really a choice after all; there are no other more stable two-legged stools. Rather, as we shall see, the choice is between the various kinds of conflicts and games you can play.

Since most people learn to have more useful conflict and play more productive games only by having more destructive conflict and less helpful games first, we'll also start there. This way, you will be a little better equipped to recognize them when they happen, and hopefully learn how to respond more appropriately.

I have already described rather vaguely the game of distancing and pursuit (or pursuit and distancing). But what does that game really look like in couples? Well, it often takes the form of criticism. If you are walking away from me, and I criticize you (pushing that button that as your spouse I know better than almost anyone), you are almost sure to take the bait and defend or justify yourself. And then I have just prevented you, at least for a little while, from going any further while we are engaged in deciding whether or not you deserve that criticism.

Or we can play the "wounded animal" game. If I curl up in a ball on the floor and act like I am helpless, you will stop and come back and help me get back on my feet again.

Or we can play the "raging lunatic" game. I act uncontrollable and you stick around to make sure I don't hurt myself.

Or we can play the "mutually assured destruction" game. I insult and hurt you so you will do the same to me so we can both feel wounded and retreat to be alone for a while.

Or we can simply play the "I'm going out for a while" game and leave without telling our partner where we are going or how long we will be gone.

The variations of the game are endless, but they all have the same purpose: to reclaim that sense of togetherness or of self when we feel one or the other to be threatened. Aren't we just awful people to do that to those we love? My answer is no, we are just people who unconsciously do awful things sometimes to make sure we don't fall over (or apart).

Please keep in mind that this kind of game-playing is done in any type of relationship and not just with our spouses. You didn't just play checkers or Parcheesi in your childhood home; you played emotional games there too. The same for your fraternity or sorority or sports team or church. And they all impact one another, as we saw in the last chapter's mother-in-law example.

Incidentally, there are other things that can be used as the third leg of a couple's stool. Children are a very stabilizing force in a marriage. You come together to take care of that new baby. A new home is a very stabilizing force. You will need to decorate it together and plant a flower garden.

The dark side of these latter examples is, of course, that these can be brought into a relationship precisely to cause more chaos. As stabilizing as children can be, they are also an endless source of conflict for a couple. That new house, with its mortgage and its upkeep or its renovation, is ideal for keeping a couple tied up in knots. And like the examples of games above, conflict is a stabilizing force in a relationship.

If you are beginning to say to yourself, "Wait, this is beginning to sound a little like that concept of triangulation," then we are making progress, because indeed it is. The purpose of triangulation is the management of anxiety, and whether it is one of your spouse's annoying habits, or one of his or her parents, or even a new job or a new pet, any of these can be used to avoid falling down (or apart).

Now, here is that happy ending. It doesn't have to be this way. And you don't even have to find replacements for conflict and game-playing to stabilize yourselves. You see, now that you understand their purpose, you only have to find healthier conflicts and games (or play the old ones better). Isn't conflict really just two ideas in the same place at the same time? And it is always good to have more options, right? Isn't every problem also an opportunity? This will be the focus of the final part of the book, but next we'll explore your role in moving in that direction.

QUESTIONS

What emotional games have you seen played in your family of origin? What conflicts? What purposes did they serve?

What conflicts or games have you been involved in outside your family? Using what you have read here, how can you understand them differently?

What are your "buttons" (those emotionally sensitive areas in your life) that your spouse might try to push in these situations?

* * *

EXERCISE

Read the classic, "Games People Play" by Eric Berne, to understand better emotional game playing.

SLEEPING ARRANGEMENTS

In the final chapter in this part on the dynamics of togetherness, I want to share an image that at once encapsulates the problem and offers a compelling and more comfortable solution.

If you have not discovered this already, you may find that sleeping in the same bed with another person, no matter how much you love him or her, does not bring you a restful night's sleep. Starting with the other person's tossing and turning during the night, their preferred sleeping position, and their greed for the blanket, and then factoring in trips to the bathroom, differing hours of laying down and getting up, and, later on, arising to tend to a crying infant or terrified toddler, beauty rest can turn into beauty risk.

One of the main reasons people toss and turn in the night is that they find their mattress to be either too soft or too firm for their needs. If this is an issue for even one of you, it causes that person to move around a lot in the middle of the night, and each time you do, it causes the spouse to move. Imagine if neither of you are comfortable with the firmness! And sooner or later you may find yourself contemplating this heart wrenching decision: do I continue to suffer together in this bed, or do I start sleeping in a separate bed. Talk about a betrayal of togetherness!

But wait! There's hope! The adjustable bed!

Yes, you too can "dial in" your ideal mattress firmness level for maximum comfort with one of these beds that offers a way to adjust each side. If you need, say, a 65 on the firmness scale and your spouse needs a 35, no problem. You don't need to continue along with either a 50 on both sides of the same bed or a 65 in one bed and a 35 in another bed. Problem solved.

As with the jam incident I shared earlier, most couples, early on in their marriage (and regrettably later on in many cases) are so emotionally stuck together that they cannot see a way out of their togetherness issues. They continue suffering through increasingly difficult conflicts thinking that they have either chosen the wrong person, or that the marriage is broken since they wouldn't be having all these problems if it wasn't. And as they continue to suffer, their patterns of relating to each other become more and more fixed, making it harder and harder to untangle. And then they come to my office hoping I can help them sort it all out and find that happiness they had when they were where you are now.

Let me re-emphasize here that I know that I am painting a kind of grim picture of marriage. But as grim as it may seem, even grimmer are those looming divorce statistics that suggest that although my description is unpleasant, it is not unrealistic. No one thinks they are going to end up on the wrong side of that 50% divide. But 50% do.

So how do you keep your marriage from meeting the Grim Reaper? By working toward doing emotionally for your marriage what an adjustable bed does for your beauty rest: to "dial in" your own needs so you can be comfortable sleeping together.

This process of emotional maturation has a name, though I hesitate to use it because it sounds so technical and clinical. But here it is: self-differentiation, and it is the ability of a person to simultaneously define (cultivate, grow) their sense of self, while always remaining in touch (contact, communion) with others. Although it sounds ridiculously simple, it is quite challenging to do. Unfortunately, you can't simply go out and buy it like an adjustable bed.

Most newlyweds struggle on the fusion end of the scale of togetherness, although some must confront the cutoff side. This concept of self-differentiation is the antidote to either extreme because it addresses both of those basic emotional needs of self and togetherness, of "I" and "We", of independence and dependence. More highly differentiated people are those who can more easily and flexibly change their own position on that continuum in response to the anxiety they experience. Less well differentiated people are those who want to make the other person change their position.

This expectation of change is a critical issue for couples at all stages of their marriage. For as long as a either partner believes that the other one must change for their problems to be resolved, or for them to find happiness, there will be a large obstacle to any kind of change actually taking place.

But when even one partner (but preferably both!) takes responsibility for changing himself or herself, whether or not the other person ever changes, there is hope and happiness on the horizon. That decision is the hardest, because it means to decide to betray your togetherness, no matter what it costs.

NO QUESTIONS OR EXERCISES!

Just take a break after this first half of the book and let it all sink in for a while!

PART 4

THE WAGON WHEEL

There is an illustration I think I have used in every single wedding homily I have ever given. It is simply that perfect. It is the humble wagon wheel.

It comes from the great Roman Catholic writer Henri Nouwen, who describes the life of faith as a wagon wheel, the center of which, the hub, is God. It is a wonderful metaphor for describing the effect our relationship with God has on our relationships with other people. If you think of each of us as occupying a spoke, we are connected to God at the hub, but also to everyone else by virtue of our connection at the common edge where the proverbial rubber meets the road. When we are at the end of our spoke, we are at a certain, fixed distance from other people, and a long way from God.

I like to remind couples that God gives us the choice whether or not to move down that spoke toward the center. The great added benefit of cultivating our relationship with God is that as we travel down toward the center, closer and closer to God, we also get closer and closer to one another, at least those who are also moving toward the center. And isn't greater, and more authentic, intimacy what we hope for with our spouse and with other people in our lives?

At the risk of committing the grave theological error of confusing God and self, let me suggest that the image also very helpfully applies if you understand the center as your humanity, or your life's project, or (put more religiously) as fulfilling God's intention for your life. By this I mean that you will only grow closer to your spouse if you are growing on your own. I believe it is the primary responsibility of each partner in a marriage to be moving toward the center, however you may wish to define that center, and no matter whether the other person is doing so or not. Ideally, you will both move along at nearly the same rate, but even if you don't, this cannot prevent either of you from moving forward. If you wait for your partner, neither of you will ever move.

Let me be clear that by moving forward, I don't mean moving away, or apart. This may be what it feels like at first. Nouwen's wagon wheel metaphor makes clear that you can't leave it all behind (unless someone breaks off your spoke); you will always be connected to others.

What I am referring to is the process of emotional maturation that makes us better people to live with, and more easily able to deal with change and anxiety. At this point in your life, you may hope that your spouse (or your parents, or anyone else) will never change, that you will be able to hold on to what seems quite perfect right now. But there are two things to say about that. The first is that it is quite impossible; if even one person in a system changes, all others will be affected somehow. (Even if nothing else happens, that non-adjustable mattress from the last chapter will only get older and lumpier, and that is change in itself.) And the second is that if nobody changes, life can get quite unbearable. You will want and need change in your life.

And so there are good reasons to be proactive in your own forward movement rather than being reactive to the change other people bring to your doorstep. Here is one.

It is a quirk of chemistry that under certain conditions, hot water will freeze faster than cold water. Like many great scientific discoveries, this one came to light accidentally, by a Ugandan high school student named Kwame Oganye who was making ice cream for a school project. Feel free to Google this fascinating story.

As a high school student, this phenomenon intrigued me, and so I asked my own chemistry teacher for its explanation, and what he told me made a lot of sense. He said that it was all about the movement of electrons, that the properties of chemical compounds change according to the movement of the electrons in the molecules. In hot water, the electrons were already moving at a faster rate than those in water at room temperature, a condition that also needed to be true for water to go from room temperature to freezing. So, he said, because the electrons in hot water were already in motion, they could move to their new positions more quickly, rather than having to start up from nothing. I believed every word.

Well, it turns out that my chemistry teacher had the right answer but for the wrong equation. Although this theory of electron movement may explain some phenomena, it does not account for hot water freezing faster than cold. But we can learn even from mistakes, and what I have learned is that although his theory is bad chemistry, it makes good sense when applied to relationships.

My point in telling you the details of this admittedly incorrect theory is for you to see that if you keep your "electrons moving" by keeping a fire lit under yourself— by always moving toward that center—you will be able to pass from one state to another more easily and quickly when plunged into a new environment. If you are already comfortable with emotional change in your own life, you will much more easily accommodate it in someone else's. And imagine how much faster you will accommodate change together if you are both already in hot water of your own making.

The next two parts of the book are about lighting that fire under yourselves that make you better to live with. Remembering that the dual aspects of this process of self-differentiation are "defining self" and "staying in touch with others," the task of part four is to help you understand what it means to "define self," what to expect when you do, and how to deal with the reaction you will receive. This defining of self needs to take place in each of your individual lives, but also your life together as a couple, a kind of self in its own right. We'll look at the "staying in touch" part in part five.

Dividing these tasks into two parts may make it sound like you have to do one before the other, but nothing could be further from the truth. As we will soon see, if you can't manage the staying connected part, you will never be able to define self (and vice versa). But we need to begin somewhere.

Finally, I want to say at this point that this process will not necessarily be only with respect to your spouse, at least not initially. You will likely need to address it first with one or both of your families as they naturally react to your blessed togetherness.

That's because you are all spokes on that great wagon wheel together.

SHARE THE ROAD, NOT YOUR ANXIETY

There is a common road sign and bumper sticker that reminds motorists to "Share the Road" with motorcycles so as to reduce the number of accidents attributed to the oft-cited lack of visibility.

Perhaps in cars, and in marriages, there ought to be a sign visible to the occupants which says, 'Share the Road, Not Your Anxiety.' You see, more wrecks happen inside of cars than out on the highway, because managing a motor vehicle is much easier than managing one's emotions while driving that vehicle when anxiety collides with inescapable togetherness.

Maybe you will recognize this typical conflict scenario many couples face. I know I have with my wife. You are driving somewhere together and traffic slows down (for no apparent reason) and the driver says, "Aaargh, I can't stand going so slow. Why are these people being so stupid?" And the other person says nothing – because they are reading or knitting or sleeping or doing something else they are perfectly happy to be doing since they are not driving. And a little while later an even more frustrated growl comes out of the driver, followed by a raised eyebrow from the passenger side of the car. And then the third time there is a snippy comment returned to the driver saying, "Don't share your poisonous atmosphere with me," and the next thing you know you are arguing about the price of milk, the Middle East peace process, or whose mother is the bigger witch.

What is happening here? Well, the driver wants the passenger to vibrate at the same frequency. That makes them feel better to have some solidarity in their suffering. But the passenger doesn't necessarily want to take on that role and the conflict ensues as the distancing and pursuing run their natural course, and the next thing you know they are in a full-blown argument until the traffic opens up again and they go unhappily on their way. And then they arrive at their destination in a foul mood and have to put on a happy face for the family or friends they have gone to visit. It is not pleasant and nobody likes to do it, but it happens all the time.

It also works the other direction too, of course, as when the proverbial backseat driver irritates the real driver by offering "helpful suggestions," observations really made because he or she is not able to manage whatever anxiety they may feel not being in control of the vehicle, whether it is a question of direction, safety, comfort, or more likely, something completely unrelated.

Why does this happen? Because as people who must "share the road" with others, we haven't learned how to take care of our own feelings about whatever might annoy us and avoid pursuing the need to have someone be on our side in the midst of our frustration.

This is the very first point at which we can begin to define ourselves: to clarify what is my responsibility and what is someone else's. Which are my feelings and which belong to the other person? Which are my beliefs and values, and which am I living out uncomfortably just to maintain my sense of balance in my family? Where do I end and where does the next person begin? What level of firmness do I need on my side of the mattress?

This can be both a very challenging and necessary task in families that tend to be more emotionally fused together, and that place a high value on family unanimity. In these families, the unwritten rules tend to be ones like, "Adult children (and their spouses) shall not live far away from the family," an example which puts an adult child in the position of having to decide just how much that rule applies to his or her own sense of self and future, and how much does it belong to the larger group. What consequences is he or she willing to accept to make such a move? Or to reject it?

This is less of an issue in families that tend toward more emotional distance, but even when individual autonomy seems like a virtue, there are still choices to make about one's self. Such a family may have an unwritten rule that certain topics (related to emotional intimacy, for example) are off limits. Part of defining yourself in this case might involve running the risk of having conversations which others are reluctant to have and, once again, bearing the consequences.

Unless you choose otherwise, these issues are more likely to come to you than you are to go to them. But if you make this kind of self-reflection a priority, you will be ahead of the curve. Simply being able to recognize the signs that you are experiencing anxiety will be a big step. Then, when you get stuck in one of life's traffic jams, you will be able to recognize that urge to rope your spouse (or children or others) into your anxiety, and choose otherwise. You will begin to think about what else is progressing so slowly in your life that slow traffic raises your anxiety to such an intolerable level that you are willing to risk a fight with your spouse, rather than work on it. You will remember that your spouse is there to share the journey, not your anxiety.

QUESTIONS

What are the "slow traffic zones" in your life right now? How have these impacted the relationship with your fiancé/fiancée?

In situations when you are anxious, what response do you want or expect from your spouse? Is this realistic?

How do you know when you are anxious? What are the physical or emotional indicators for you?

* * *

EXERCISE

Prepare a personal mission and/or vision statement. For mission, answer the question, "Who am I?" For vision, "Where am I going (or where is God leading me)?

SELFISH IS NOT A FOUR LETTER WORD

From as early as you had awareness of a brother or sister, or entered school, you have been bombarded with messages about sharing–share your toys, your books, maybe even your bedroom. Don't be selfish! Share!

And religion generally reinforces that virtue. Be selfless rather than selfish. Don't live for yourself. Live for others. Give and do not expect a reward.

This is all very good wisdom. The world would be a pitiable place without sharing and selfless giving.

And yet, one of the most commonly heard expressions from at least one partner in a marital crisis is that he or she feels they have lost themselves in the relationship, that they no longer know who they are. They never have enough time for themselves, to read a book or to go for a walk, pursue a hobby, etc. Their boundaries are blurred. They feel like a number or a robot.

My observation about such situations is that one or both partners have lost sight of the fact that selfish is not a bad word, at least not if the pursuit is of identity, purpose, health, authenticity, or balance, to name just a few of the treasures that spending time on yourself can uncover. Too often these precious gems are sacrificed for "the sake of the relationship" rather than valued for the beauty and richness they bring into our lives. But such gems are irreplaceable, and both partners bear the cost of selling or giving them away.

It is never selfish to spend time learning who you are, or what gifts you possess, or in what direction you want to go in life. In fact, you could say that it is selfish to suspend this effort since it will rob your marriage of all the benefits this knowledge and experience brings. And yet, couples all too frequently express that to pursue their own individuality seems like a betrayal of their partnership.

It is one of the most commonly used clichés of television sitcoms to have a couple come into conflict because the husband wants to play poker, or go fishing, or hang out at the bar with his buddies. He is accused of abandoning his wife, and made to feel guilty that he has friends who mean something to him. And so they argue, and he storms out to meet with his friends, but of course, he is now tormented with anxiety about his wife's feelings. And so he leaves early to the scorn of his buddies, returns home chastened, and apologizes to his wife, having learned his lesson about hearth and home. They live happily ever after—in TV land.

In real life, this couple will be divorced in five years, or stay together and suffer indefinitely until one of the partners grows a spine. In TV land, that would get the show cancelled.

Please do not think I am blaming women for family conflict by using the stereotype of nagging wives who browbeat their husbands. That example is simply so well-known that almost everyone will be able to recognize it. In real life, the pressure to abandon individual interests and pursuits gets played out in countless ways, affecting men and women alike, and always having the devastating effect of helping bring about a loss of self in one or both of the partners which will lead them into even greater anxiety and unwanted conflict.

The television example also illustrates the common misunderstanding that one person is to blame. At first glance, it appears that the husband is the wrong kind of selfish and weak, and that the wife is virtuous. He is selfish in wanting to spend time away from his wife, yet also weak because he is not true to his convictions and returns home. But what is often overlooked is that the wife is also selfish and weak. She is selfish in denying her husband the opportunity of his own pursuits, possibly because she is not being selfish enough in her own pursuits. And she is weak for staying home and moping when she could be feeding her own spirit in whatever way she finds meaningful. Neither of them have a spine.

When you get married, you do not stop having friends, or enjoying bowling or reading. You may sleep in the same bed, but you still each have different dreams in that bed. You do not suddenly begin having the same favorite jam. You do not wake up the next morning with the same political or religious views as your spouse. This is all as it should be. And it is perfectly acceptable, and maybe even essential, to fight for it.

This is probably the most significant challenge you will face: to try to be always moving forward each in your own right in the midst of being a couple. I cannot emphasize enough that each of you needs to be as selfish as it takes to be the best person you can be, physically, emotionally, spiritually, professionally, and in any other way that is important for your authentic sense of self. I do hope it goes without saying that you need to do this in a balanced way that honors your relationship. In the end, the best wedding gift you can give your spouse is to be as clear about who you are on your own as you are as a couple.

QUESTIONS

What aspects of your single life are you worried might get sacrificed for the sake of your marriage? How problematic would it be for you if they were?

Even before getting married, how selfish (in the positive sense) would you say you are? How clear would you say you are on who you are? How you want to pursue your life?

What are your sources of inspiration for your life's direction?

* * *

EXERCISE

Write a "profile" of your sense of self five years from now. Answer it in the form of completing the statement, "If I felt perfectly balanced between self and couple, I would have (done, felt, etc.) _____. Be as specific as you can.

On Rocking the Boat

At some point, you will decide that some additional self-definition is a good thing, and that you'd like to give it a try. Of course, you've already done it at various stages of your life, but probably more or less unconsciously. You carved out some territory amongst your siblings, got a little more freedom from your parents, took a few risks, and so on.

But the change you are thinking about making now is a little more calculated, more on the surface of your awareness. You know you need to create a little distance from your parents who can't resist the urge to call the newlyweds every few days and offer their unsolicited, and frankly, unwanted advice that makes you feel even more incompetent than you already feel.

But as you think about ways you could break it to them, none of them seem gentle enough. And so you begin to say to yourself that, well, it's not really so bad, and they have been married for thirty years, so maybe they have something to offer. But as the calls begin to make you more and more anxious (and you realize this because you have reflected on why your spouse is suddenly annoying you more often…), you realize that you really will have to let them know. So you pick up the phone…and then put it down again, thinking, "I really don't want to disappoint them." And the drama continues.

Our decisions for change are frequently never realized because of our fears. We worry that we will hurt another person's feelings, or cause their health to deteriorate, or create a family rift, and so we back off. We don't want to rock the boat, as the old saying goes. But inside you, the waves are threatening to swamp your ship, and it is taking on water.

Here is what you need to know about those people you are worried about hurting. They are really not as fragile as you think. You may indeed rock their boat, but it is very unlikely that it will tip over, and if it does, it is because they were poor sailors and not because the waves you created were so huge.

This is to say that it is very helpful to recognize the distinction between hurting people and damaging them, between an emotional cut on the finger and the amputation of a limb. This is the insight of Rabbi Edwin Friedman in his book, "A Failure of Nerve," who noted that we tend to overestimate the effects of our self-differentiation and underestimate the emotional resiliency of the people affected by our changes. These combine to paralyze us into inaction through the mistaken belief that the other party will not be able to overcome the blow we give them.

But, Friedman says, it is very, very difficult to damage someone when we are simply defining self. You are not defining self when you belittle someone else, or tell them they are worthless. That is damaging behavior. But by their very nature, sincere efforts at personal change cannot possibly be directed at making other people feel bad, since they are efforts at helping ourselves to function better.

Your uncomfortable conversation with your parents asking them to back off a little will very likely hurt their feelings. They may even offer a comeback that will hurt your feelings (and we'll take a look at that dynamic in the next couple of chapters). But if your parents go and throw themselves off a bridge because you asked them to call you less frequently, or to change the topic of conversation, they have bigger problems than your request, for which they alone bear responsibility, and there's nothing you can do about that in any event.

The instinct to protect people we care about from information that may upset them is a noble one. But nobility is overrated. The truth in these situations is that the real instinct at work is the one for self-protection, so that we do not have to be affected by another person's feelings, or so we can protect our less than helpful self-image. We employ that instinct to avoid situations in which we feel anxious, and we have explored what we usually then go and do with that anxiety. We are far more likely to damage people by involving them in an anxiety-shifting triangle than by speaking our truth to their face.

The same distinction between hurting and damaging is helpful to remember when we are on the receiving end of another person's efforts at self-definition. This insight may help us receive their words to us less defensively, because we have learned that there is not as much at stake as we first believed. If we curl up in a ball, or strike back, that is our responsibility, not the person who has just spoken their truth to us.

So go ahead and pick up that telephone and say your piece. Quite likely, your parents will be relieved that you finally removed the burden of responsibility they were feeling about supporting you in those early weeks of your marriage. Often, the truth we think will hurt or damage someone else is the truth that sets them, and us, free. Funny how we are connected like that...

QUESTIONS

Can you recall a time when speaking the truth about yourself hurt someone? Damaged someone?

What are some of the family dynamics you feel least prepared to approach? Best prepared?

How have you seen this kind of self-sabotage at work in your own life?

* * *

EXERCISE

The next time you need to speak to someone about an uncomfortable topic, rehearse it in the mirror beforehand. This will let you hear out loud if your words have the potential to actually damage someone.

THEY *WILL* COME FOR YOU

When I work with someone who has decided to make a change with the goal of more clearly defining self in a problematic relationship, I always make sure to remind them of two things. The first is that before it gets better, it will get worse. The second is that the change is the easy part. Sticking with the change in the face of emotional sabotage is the vastly more challenging part.

One of my favorite books is by the late British travel writer Eric Newby called "When the Snow Comes They Will Take You Away." It is his autobiographical account of both his time as a prisoner of war in Italy during World War Two and how he met the love of his life, Wanda. Newby and several others escaped from their prison camp and fled to the Apennine hills in northern Italy. Newby was fortunate enough to be discovered by Wanda and her family who helped him to survive by hiding him in the countryside and bringing him food each day while he was stuck unable to get back across enemy lines.

The title of the book refers to Wanda's lament, as they realized they were falling in love, that their days together would be numbered. Winter was coming, and with it, the growing impossibility of resupplying him with food without their activity being discovered. The tracks in the snow would lead the Italian soldiers right to him to be recaptured. This is exactly what happened and Newby was returned to his POW camp until the end of the war. Yes, he and Wanda were reunited and lived happily ever after.

Wanda knew how important it was to the Italian army that they not let their security breach go unpunished. They were not simply going to let him get away with his emancipation without a struggle. Neither will your families.

I realize when describing family process that it may sound like I think all families are full of overbearing, dark-hearted tyrants who will use any means necessary, including treachery and emotional blackmail, to control every aspect of their subjects' lives.

None of that is true—except the part about emotional blackmail. This is the family equivalent of Newton's second law of physics, that every emotional action will be met with an equal and opposite reaction. It is how families maintain their equilibrium, no matter how healthy or unhealthy that equilibrium may be. You saw in the last chapter how it is even self-imposed at times when we get paralyzed by worry about hurting others.

Imagine that you, your spouse, and another person have been charged with the responsibility to keep a rope from touching the ground using only your bodies and that if the rope touches the ground, calamity will strike. Now, imagine what will happen when one person takes a step inward, perhaps because he or she has decided to risk calamity or just got tired of the responsibility. One or both of the other people will move themselves to pick up the slack created by that step forward. The rope will tighten up again and the universe is safe once more, again and again, until the end of time.

Change is not impossible however. It will simply require more effort than you had imagined. In the next chapter we will see how you can persevere in making these changes, but for now, it is important to be able to recognize emotional sabotage when it comes, because they *will* come for you.

This unconscious emotional sabotage comes in an endless variety of forms, some more direct than others, but all designed to make you doubt the wisdom of the decision you have made.

- It may come in the form of concerned comments about your appearance or your weight (when you have decided there are more important changes to make).

- It may come as criticism about the behavior of your children (which implies that you are not raising them according to family tradition).

- It may come as behavioral brush fires you will need to put out so the forest doesn't burn down (so that you will be too busy to finish that project that earns you that promotion).

- It may come in the form of your own body's rebellion through tiredness or illness (because our bodies are systems needing balance too).

The single most important thing to remember when faced by emotional sabotage is that it is natural and normal. No one is trying to hurt you. They are trying to protect themselves and the larger family's integrity. Your change implies their change, and even if their own change might be beneficial, our first reaction to change is almost always to oppose it.

A final great irony about change is that when you finally make a change that others have pushed you to make, they will still resist it! Why? Because the dynamic of your resistance to their suggestions has been an important factor in keeping that rope from falling to the ground.

QUESTIONS

Have you experienced this kind of resistance to change, either in your own life or the lives of others?

How have you resisted change in other people's lives?

What is your family's "calamity" that would occur if it let the rope drop? Is it real or imaginary?

* * *

EXERCISE

Try the rope exercise with other people. Don't let them know what will happen. Remember: no hands!

JUST WALK ON IT — IT WILL BE OK

After the first time I dropped out of college, I lived and worked with a guy named Chuck who was one of the funniest people I've ever known. He was a walking repository of one-liners and his best one was delivered whenever someone complained about some rather vague or mild ache or pain, especially when it came with a hint that the injured party might have to miss work. He'd say, "Looks like we'll have to amputate at the neck." Far from the saying that "Idle hands are the devil's workshop," Chuck knew well that the idleness that really mattered was located in the mind.

Chuck's advice will serve you well when dealing with resistance to change. Just cut off your head. It will only get in the way. You can't think your way out of the resistance. You just have to keep walking forward. But even then, it might not be enough.

Then you can use one of my mother's sayings that also applies. Whenever one of us children would lay on the ground writhing in agony over what we believed was a broken ankle, or at least a torn ligament suffered walking somewhere we didn't want to go, she would say, "Just walk on it for a while. It will be OK." And it always was.

The best antidote to resistance to change is perseverance. If you give up in the face of opposition, you lose. You just have to keep on trying. This sounds simple, but I cannot tell you how many people I know who have abandoned their efforts at making change because they could not persevere long enough to see them through.

There is a drawing I have that I use to remind myself, and others, to persevere. It is of a frog almost entirely swallowed up by a heron. But with its feet still dangling out, the frog has its hands squeezed around the neck of the bird keeping its throat too constricted to let itself be swallowed. It is captioned, "Don't ever give up!"

Let us return to our example of your parents' too frequent phone calls offering unwanted advice. It is possible that your first brushoff would be a polite, "Thanks for the advice," thinking that affirmation will be enough to get them off your back. But they call again.

And so you try to convince them that really, everything is going great, and that they don't need to worry. But they call again. You decide not to answer when you see their number show up on the caller ID. They now call more frequently and you begin to think they are stalkers. Can't they figure it out?

When you finally decide to answer, they express worry over your lack of response, sure that you are avoiding them because you are too embarrassed to share your troubles with them. With the most compassionate voices possible, they have advice for that too.

You are now officially ready to give up and resign yourself to having to either endlessly endure these conversations or not answer the phone for a few weeks at a time. You give thanks that they do not yet know how to send you text messages.

But then you remember the drawing of the frog and you decide not only to persevere but also to try a new tactic. You decide to tell them the truth, that their advice, however well intended, is making you feel uncomfortable. Would they please stop or change the topic of the conversation? They agree, but not before giving you some advice on how to lower your monthly telecommunications bill. You think you have finally gotten your point across. Then they call again.

Now you are almost at the point of screaming at them to stop, but you remember a book that advised you to persevere at all costs, and so you try another new approach. You begin to offer them advice, since your marriage is going so well and you are learning so much. You begin to call them every day with a new nugget of wisdom. You ask about their marriage, and how it is going. Soon enough, their calls taper off and you realize you have all reached a new equilibrium.

What is important here is not that you have turned the tables and won. It is that in the process of defining yourself, you have learned how to control your own anxiety when talking to your parents. Because the real perseverance we are talking about is in your own emotional growth. You have managed your own emotions in a way that has communicated to them that their baby really is grown up after all (and that they can now turn their attention to their own relationship!). It shouldn't take so much effort, I know, but it often does.

The trick to this kind of perseverance is not simply to try and try again. It is to keep in mind the old truism that "the only person you can change is yourself," knowing that when you change, everyone else must too. You won't need to emotionally manipulate others, just to manage yourself.

QUESTIONS

When have you successfully persevered to accomplish something? When haven't you succeeded? What can you learn from these experiences?

How do you perceive your family's overall openness to change? How do you rate their emotional flexibility? Your own?

Have you found yourself positively changed through another person's efforts at change?

* * *

EXERCISE

Find a saying or image (like my drawing of the frog and the heron) that you can use as inspiration for perseverance. Put it up somewhere you can't avoid it.

PART 5

TOWARD A MORE PERFECT UNION

"Where there's death, there's hope." That was a favorite saying of a priest friend of mine whenever she found herself dealing with difficult people. Mind you, she said this in the kindest, most Christian way possible. And she really was one of the most compassionate, graceful people I have ever known. It is just that even someone as patient as her can reach the end of her rope.

In the last part, we looked a little more closely at one of the twin challenges of self-differentiation, the defining of self. In this part we will look at the other, the staying in touch with others. In many ways, this is the harder part of the equation, at least in western societies that place a high premium on personal independence. We have, in many ways, become experts in defining self, and even better at simply cutting off those with whom we cannot seem to have a harmonious relationship. We just move on, farther west, to an undiscovered country. Perhaps this accounts for the high divorce rate. It is at least a significant factor.

Compared to emotional fusion, cutoff happens rather quickly and intentionally. Few people decide to enter into a fused kind of relationship. They just can't see how they are growing together into emotionally conjoined twins until they can no longer get out of their own side of the bed. But many people deliberately seek to create distance in the hope that it will reduce conflict. If I am farther away, the thinking goes, that other person can't affect me. So we simply turn our backs, or burn our bridges, or offer a cold shoulder, and find relief. The problem with this thinking is that while there may be less direct conflict, there is no less anxiety in either person. It is simply directed now to other relationships. As I observed earlier in the book, your place in a family, or any kind of system, does not just disappear because you do. And neither does your anxiety.

One of the reasons staying connected (or getting reconnected) is challenging is that it requires a certain kind of humility, of admitting that cutoff is a bad idea, and submitting to the harder work of dealing with issues more honestly and directly. Saving face is hard while eating humble pie. Sticking around seems to be showing the cards in your hand too soon, giving the other person the edge. You are as much as admitting this relationship means enough to you that you are willing to risk getting your heart stomped on again.

But staying in touch is not about mending fences for their own sake or keeping the peace or sacrificing yourself for the good of the family. It is about being able to come to terms with the anxiety between you so that it does not eat away at either of you and cause chaos in other places in your life. As with defining self, the trick is to be able to manage your own anxiety well enough to change appropriately your behavior in a problematic relationship without giving it up. You are changing your perspective on that relationship, for your own sake.

Let me offer an illustration that at first might sound odd, but that has a wonderful significance that grows on you. Most people are unnerved by the prospect of death, and even more so by its bodily reality. Bones and blood just creep a lot of people out. We keep our physical and emotional distance from them.

But in the great monasteries of Mount Athos in Greece, the center of the spirituality of the Eastern Orthodox Christian tradition, the monks have a profoundly meaningful practice to deal simultaneously with death and life, with past, present and future, and with self and other. When one of the monks dies, he is buried. But after a certain number of years, when the body has decomposed such that only the bones remain, it is dug up, and those bones are added to the collection of the bones of all of the monks that have gone before him. So there is an area on the monastery grounds where you can walk by and see great piles of the pelvises and shoulder blades and femurs of monks from the last several hundred years. Please do not try this in your backyard.

Some of the monasteries even have a small building in which the skulls of the monks are displayed with numbers written on the forehead, so that they can be identified. For the monastic community, these are places they can go to remember how profoundly connected they are with the past, but also how profoundly alive they are right now. They can remember the wisdom of the generations that have gone before them, and realize that it is their turn now to pass on that wisdom. This is a brutally honest, if graphic, way of recognizing the link between self and others. It is also a great way to remember that whatever mistakes their brethren made in the past need not necessarily live on in the present.

Self-differentiating is like developing the capacity to not only write the poetry of your heart, or to do your exercise routine, or to practice the piano, or anything else quite personal and vulnerable, but to do those things in a roomful of people who all have something to say about it, (or maybe just a roomful of their bones) and neither give up your efforts, or freak out and run away. You will have to deal with those people at the same time you are dealing with your own mind, body, or spirit. Either that, or run away and join a monastery. But be forewarned that monasteries are their own kind of family too, with all the same issues I have been describing all along.

That is to say that, metaphorically speaking, when we think about moving forward with our lives, we would just as soon leave the problematic people in our lives right where they were originally buried, off in some distant cemetery, and perhaps visit the gravesite once a year and leave some flowers, rather than digging them up and putting them nearby in a proper, respectful place. And yet, leaving them buried only leaves half our work incomplete.

On a day-to-day basis, the ability to stay connected must work hand in hand with the defining of self. When you try to do one without the other, people start freaking out, and that is never a helpful way to accomplish your goal of adjusting the emotional distance between you.

I should note that this business of self-differentiation applies both to your marriage and to each of you individually. In general, it is not a good idea to speak for your partner. But there will be times when you need to stand as one, and either define your twosome more clearly, or connect it more closely with other people or groups. One such occasion is the holidays, a classic wrestling match for couples when there are divided loyalties. Not only will you need to clarify everything between you, but communicate your indivisibility to the other parties involved. Holiday anxiety is bad enough on its own; it doesn't need the help of spousal betrayal.

ELIMINATE THE MIDDLEMAN

I f you already have an enduring, positive, honest, direct relationship with everyone in your future spouse's family (and your own!), I am so happy for you. If there is no one with whom you have trouble spending time, or can't cry on their shoulder, run for public office or give the rest of us lessons.

But for the other 99% of the people reading this chapter, there is someone over there on the other side of the family who just really doesn't work for you, who gets under your skin, whose intensity or rudeness or politeness scares you. These are the people you avoid at holiday parties, and when they call for your spouse, you put the phone down to go look for him or her even when he or she is within earshot. You just don't want to spend time with weird Uncle Larry.

The good news is that if weird Uncle Larry is not a key player in your spouse's family, you probably won't need to change the nature of your relationship with him to avoid problems down through the years. But if the person (or persons) in your spouse's family that you avoid are in significant positions with respect to your spouse (or later, your children), it is only a matter of time before that emotional distance gets played out in ways that will cause distress between you and your spouse.

Maybe you will experience a variation of this classic conflict. Your father-in-law (we'll give the mothers a break here) has, in your view, a really annoying way of speaking to you, like he is tolerating you only because you are the choice of his child's life partner. He makes comments to you that seem like he is mocking you, or possibly even threatening you. To him, your course of study in college, and your job prospects for the future, are dubious. He thinks your pre-marriage friends are weird. You wonder how your wonderful new bride or groom could have come forth from this man's loins.

Unless you are a real glutton for emotional punishment, chances are you will avoid him. You will find reasons to go to the store when he is scheduled to come by, or let his call go to voicemail if he calls when your spouse is not at home. When your spouse calls to wish him a Happy Birthday and hands you the phone to do the same, you mumble quick well wishes, followed by "Sorry, gotta go."

Here's the problem. Your mutual lack of affection for each other cannot possibly remain your own little secret. Other people will become involved. What normally happens is that your spouse will feel trapped in the middle of this dynamic because both of you will talk to him or her about the other one instead of talking directly. He will complain about you, and you will complain about him, and your poor spouse who loves you both will be left to defend both of your reputations in another of those nasty but normal triangles.

This is an awful role to hand off to someone and it will only come back to bite you. You do not want to put your spouse in a position to take sides or choose between you, or be some kind of mediator. This will only cause his or her anxiety to rise and bring the two of you into conflict.

This is why, from the very beginning, it is wise to eliminate the middleman (or middlewoman) and establish direct one-to-one relationships with all the key people in your spouse's family (and even in other systems like work, if possible) rather than let these flow through your spouse. A relationship doesn't even need to be problematic (like the example I used) for misunderstanding to occur. What should be a simple exchange of information between two people can share both misinformation and bad blood when you add in an unnecessary third party. Remember that old game of "Telephone Line"? Now add in an emotional component and see how much fun it is.

Please do not misunderstand me. I am not suggesting that you need to become best buddies with people you'd rather freeze out. But you will need to have a functional, non-anxious (or at least less anxious) relationship with them that does not depend on others. You will need to stay connected to them in ways that allow you to remain true to yourself, but that do not depend on the other person to change. Because they may never change (more on that later).

Yes, your spouse will have to manage his or her own role in the middle, but this is primarily your responsibility, because even if he or she figures out how to avoid feeling trapped, that anxiety will remain and get worked out somewhere else. Leaving it unresolved means you run the risk of becoming emotionally distant from more people than you already are.

Like it or not, marriage imposes new relationships on you that you might not have established otherwise. What was true about your own family, that you didn't get to pick them, becomes true of your in-laws as well. You may be stuck with them too now, but eliminating the middleman allows you to make the best of that reality.

QUESTIONS

With whom in your future spouse's family do you feel less connected? Most connected? Why?

How would you rate your ability to remain calm in the midst of conflict?

What are the ways you normally use when forging a relationship with someone? Do you think these will work with your spouse's family?

* * *

EXERCISE

Have a date night together and watch the film, "Meet the Parents." Discuss!

IN CASE OF HEART ATTACK,
CHECK YOUR OWN PULSE FIRST

There is a good reason why it is not recommended to run into a burning building to rescue your belongings. You will most likely get burned, or overcome by smoke. So why on earth should you run toward someone with whom you are feeling conflicted, as I suggested in the last chapter? You will most likely get burned there too, or overcome with the emotional equivalent of smoke.

Well, I never said you should run in unprepared, did I? After all, trained firefighters enter burning buildings all the time, and they usually come back out again in one piece. That's because they have the right equipment and training to get in and get out before the ceiling caves in on them. In this chapter, we'll look more closely at how to be prepared to enter into potentially "dangerous" emotional situations and come out (more or less) unscathed.

Yes, it is daunting to contemplate running into conflict instead of running away from it, which is the natural tendency of everyone without a self-destructive streak. This is why I suggested earlier that defining self may be the easier of the twin tasks of self-differentiation. The metaphor is not perfect either. It is not your job to run in and save anyone from anything, including themselves. But the burning building metaphor does seem to capture what seems like an unavoidable risk in staying connected.

The sense of emergency is actually a good place to begin, since the very nature of anxiety makes us feel like the situation is far worse than it really is. When anxious, we go into crisis mode, and without training in crisis management, we are more likely to make things worse. So let's look at a couple of well-known nuggets of crisis management wisdom.

The first is this: in case of heart attack, check your own pulse first. When our adrenaline kicks in, because we've seen an accident, or because someone has just put a diamond ring in front of us, or because our father-in-law can't seem to deal with reality, our first reaction is just that: a reaction. It is not well thought out. It is instinctive. Adrenaline fuels that fight, flight, or freeze mechanism that is supposed to help us survive. That may work in the wilderness, but not so well in relationships.

The more appropriate step following an adrenaline-inducing impulse is to formulate a response rather than a reaction. This takes presence of mind, and the ability to calm oneself enough to review options. This is the temperament that makes sure that one's own house is in order before it tries to help another's. It is also exceedingly difficult. Staying connected requires steady hands, and a slow and regular heartbeat.

The second is like the first. There is a good reason why the preflight instructions on airplanes tell you that in the event of a loss of cabin pressure, when the oxygen masks fall from the ceiling, put your own mask on first before trying to assist others. You will not help anyone else passed out on the floor yourself. But equipped, you may be able to help many people, including yourself.

All of this is to say that when you are faced with the need to connect with someone, and your gut tells you that you may come out bruised up or barely breathing, the main resources you need are always within your grasp:

presence of mind and the ability to respond rather than react.

The presence of mind you need can perhaps be best seen in the challenge presented by the following wisdom of Rabbi Edwin Friedman: focus on the emotional process, not the content. In an anxious situation, if you have not checked your own pulse or put on your own mask, you are more likely to react to criticism than you are to respond to what's really going on emotionally between the two of you. This will be true with your spouse, in-laws, or anyone else.

Most people in this situation react defensively and start flinging facts to back up their positions, or bring out timelines of who did what to whom when. All this does is focus the conflict on a level that not even a judge and jury could sort out. What is worse is that it leaves the relationship unresolved.

But when you can keep in mind what is at stake for you in the process of connecting with someone, it is much easier to avoid being ensnared in a fruitless argument. And when you can be present in these situations in a way that also affirms what's at stake for the other person, you have an even better chance at making some progress.

What might your father-in-law fear about you? Why does it bother you so much that he criticizes you? Where do you want this relationship to end up? How do you handle more deftly your interactions without wanting to strike back? These are the questions you want to be addressing, not whether your career path, your friends, or your hairstyle are ever going to meet his standards.

QUESTIONS

Can you recall an argument you had recently? At what level did the argument take place? Content or emotional process?

What are ways you have learned to keep calm during a crisis? Keep your wits about you?

Who do you know that is emotionally "quick on their feet," able to respond rather than react? Which of their characteristics could you adopt?

* * *

EXERCISE

Ask other people whom you find emotionally mature how they deal with difficult people. Do their ideas match up with what you've read here?

THE HARDEST TASK

I've described a lot of tough assignments already in this book: honest self-evaluation, family reckoning, self-mastery, emotional maturity, and meeting conflict head-on, among others. All of these will be challenging hills even to an experienced climber.

But none of them will be as difficult as the Mount Everest of emotional peaks for couples: staying appropriately connected to your spouse when he or she *simply won't change!*

I doubt you are willing to admit it at this point, but it is almost certain that somewhere in your heart you harbor a hope that your spouse will change some aspect of his or her behavior, worldview, cleanliness, sexual appetite, or something else that maybe even already is unconsciously causing friction between you.

So, right this very minute, set down this book, look deep inside yourself, find that hope, and squash it like a bug. Repeat as necessary. (In fact, do this for the hopes you have about anyone's change…)

Don't get me wrong. As a pastor, I am in the hope business. I try to nurture it every day and help people bring it out of the hidden recesses of their imaginations into the light of day where it can be a blessing to others. But the hope that someone else, especially one's spouse, will change, is a hope that over time turns into an emotional tug of war that you can never win no matter how many people you employ on your side of the rope. You see, the other end of the rope is tied around an immoveable object. You will only end up with very tired arms and a very weary spirit.

This is not to say that your spouse is incapable of change. Far from it. In fact, his or her change is inevitable. It just may not be the change you have in mind, and it won't come because you tried to make it happen. The only way to see your desire for change take place in your spouse is if you scratch it off of your to-do list.

In fact, the more you try to change another person, the more they will resist you. And if you think about it, you should be glad this is true. Do you really want to be with someone you can mold and shape emotionally (or even behaviorally) at your whim? Would you want to change yourself under those circumstances?

Here's why this is so challenging. Again, whether we want to admit it or not, we believe deep down that if our spouse really loved us, he or she would do whatever it takes to make us happy or meet our emotional needs, including change. The person we love should love us more than his or her own self, right? After all, isn't that how we feel about them? This validates our love and our choice of them as a lifelong mate. This is that self-interested love we struggle to move past.

If we persist in that belief that our spouse should change according to our needs, we continue to breed more and more anxiety, as our love is called into question. We persist in our efforts to change the other person, find those efforts rebuffed, and often experience a withdrawal by our partner. So we try harder. And so do they. And over time we will gradually grow closer to that desire for change, and grow farther away from our spouse. The need for change becomes more important than the relationship. If we keep this up long enough, we will find ourselves struggling with that uninterested form of love. One or both of us will become so exhausted from the struggle that we will give up, or give in. There is no victory in this scenario, except for the lawyer.

There is, of course, that middle road of disinterested love, but it is the rockiest, and most convoluted path of the three. On that path, we replace the hopes we have of our spouse's change with the hopes we have for our own change. We remember that our emotional maturity does not depend on anyone else's and that we cannot wait for the other person to make the first move. We give up the emotional hostage taking that demands the ransom of change for the promise of intimacy. If we can do that, usually what happens is that during the time we have kept our own heads down, focusing on our own changes, our spouse has also changed even though we didn't see it taking place. We were disinterested enough to allow it to happen, and it did.

You *will* try to change your spouse. And he or she *will* try to change you. The hardest task of all is to stay appropriately connected to your spouse when he or she resists your efforts and seems to move away from you emotionally. When you are disappointed, and you will be, you will need to break out those crisis management techniques of presence of mind, and the ability to respond rather than react. These will help you to neither pursue nor run away, but instead to focus on how you, rather than your spouse, can change.

That is *really* staying connected. It's Mount Everest, but it's worth the climb.

QUESTIONS

How easily do you change when others push (or try to convince) you to change? How well has it worked when you have tried to persuade others?

What changes do you want to see in your own life? What changes do you fear making? Look forward to making?

What changes do you hope your spouse will make? Can you live with it if he or she can't or won't change? How will you manage your anxiety if no change comes?

* * *

EXERCISE

Do a little review of the way you have changed during your life. What commonalities surface? What motivation have you needed?

MAKING SEX WORK

On second thought, I've changed my mind. You are an exceptional couple, in more ways than one. None of the pitfalls I have described will ever happen to you. You won't even have to try very hard. It will just come naturally for you.

And as an exceptional couple, the same will be true for your sex life. It will never want for passion, creativity, time, importance, or just plain bliss.

You see what I am doing, don't you? I've stopped trying to convince you how hard marriage is. That's because we've come to the sex part, and that's easy enough. I mean, if there is one part of your life that should never seem like you have to labor at it, it is sex, right? Your romantic love for each other should pour forth naturally into mutually satisfying physical love. It's not work: It's play!

Oh, how I hope you really are that exceptional! Because most couples who want good sex (whatever "good sex" ends up meaning for them) have to make sex work. Staying connected sexually is so much harder than we think it should be.

Of course, I mean "work" in two different senses. The first is that you have to make it work in terms of function. It has to actually happen, and there's no guarantee of that happening naturally or regularly when you factor in work, stress, menstruation, children, etc. It has to have a beneficial significance to both of you. It has to avoid becoming a point of contention between you. But all in all, yes, sex can work.

But to get there (or stay there, or get back there) you have to work at it. Intentionally. Sometimes painfully, as research has so thoroughly shown. Sometimes it will need to be work in the sense of having to schedule it or prioritize it. But more often, and more to the point, it will be doing the emotional work behind the scenes to make sure it has a chance to flow more naturally. Remember that sex is one of the Big Three, and it's not up there solely on the basis of infidelity. It's that high on the list because it is not as natural as the hormones in our bodies suggests it is.

For better or worse, sex in our time is complicated. If we now perceive sex (as compared to, say, one hundred years ago), to be as much a means by which a couple can connect emotionally as physically, this opens the door for great possibilities as well as great heartbreak. If we are now able to have sex without the same social constraints related to childbearing, this gives rise to both the joy of freedom and spontaneity and the frustration of unexplainable restraint. If we are now having one or more other sexual partners before marriage, those encounters (and the unavoidable comparisons with one's spouse) add experience that can be both valuable and problematic.

It is likely that as sex has become more emotionally important to us, it has also more frequently become a painful chokepoint in marriages. Nevertheless, every problem is simultaneously an opportunity. Precisely because sex is such an emotional factor in our lives, we can actually use it as a sort of barometer for the overall health of the relationship. Sex therapist and researcher David Schnarch has made a good case showing how frequently sexual issues in a relationship are related to other aspects of the couple's functioning. In its simplest form, when things are going well overall in your relationship, your sex will be better, and vice versa.

While this might seem like perhaps the most obvious statement yet shared in this book, you would be surprised how often couples will identify problems in their sex life, but fail to own up to them in other areas. It is only when unpacking the sexual issues, Schnarch says, that larger relationship issues begin to take the precedence they deserve.

I believe this is because a couple's sex life is so easy to triangle when anxiety is high. Because it is so symbolic of togetherness, it is easy to find fault with it when togetherness has become an issue. Because it is so highly desired a marital commodity, when one partner withholds sex, the lack of sex quickly becomes the issue rather than what may be behind the decision to avoid intimacy. (Ironically, having a lot of sex can also help you avoid issues. You can convince yourself that everything is fine emotionally since your escapist sex life is so good.)

Sex then is yet another opportunity to practice the self-differentiation I have been suggesting will be a help in every area of your marriage. By clarifying your own sexual identity in mind, body, and spirit (knowing your own body and its sexual response, coming to terms with body image, previous sexual experiences or trauma, or family or religious beliefs about sex, among others) and staying connected to your spouse sexually (not withholding sex for dubious purposes or avoiding or rejecting those parts of your partner's sexual identity you find anxiety-producing, among others) you have a greater chance of cultivating a sex life that is emotionally as well as physically gratifying.

QUESTIONS

What are your beliefs about sex? Emotionally? Physically?
How important is it to you? How much have you really
explored your feelings on the subject?

How did your family and/or religious tradition view sex?
Was it out in the open? Taboo?

What hopes or fears about sex do you bring to your
marriage? For what questions do you still need answers?

* * *

EXERCISE

If you feel your sexual IQ is lower than you would like
heading into your marriage, take some time and read up, or
find someone whose advice on the subject your trust, and
ask them some questions.

The Strangest Musical Instrument
of Them All

It is a common complaint among partners a little later on in their marriages that they have begun to feel disconnected from one another. They will describe a pace of life, or a career trajectory, or other factors that leave them feeling a little like astronauts on a spacewalk— connected to the mother ship, but floating around and hanging on by a thread.

This is normal. You will survive it. It need not be a crisis. And it will not be a crisis if you intentionally cultivate that practice of "staying in touch" that I have been describing. In fact, the wisest couples will use those seasons of separateness to spend the necessary time on self, because they have the blessed assurance of a bond that cannot be broken. Instead of reacting to the distance they feel by rushing blindly toward the other person with their arms wide open screaming, "Love me!", a wise partner will respond to it by taking advantage of the opportunity to nurture that greater sense of self which makes them ever more attractive to their spouse, a factor in more naturally drawing the other closer to them again. That wise partner will do something really useful with that time. Like learn to play the accordion.

The accordion is the perhaps the strangest musical instrument in the world, and one of the most beautiful (when played by an expert!). It can accompany other instruments and help guide polka dancers, but it can also evoke the deepest emotions of longing and joy as a solo instrument. It is also a great image for a healthy marriage.

The accordion has two keyboards connected by a set of pleated bellows. These keyboards are not the same. One is laid out like a traditional piano, but the other is a grid of buttons. Each requires a different style of fingering to bring forth its unique but complementary sound.

But neither side can make even a note of music without what connects them in the middle. As the bellows are expanded and contracted by moving the keyboards together and apart, they draw air into the instrument and push it out again through the keyboard chambers to produce the notes you hear. But if the keyboards can't work without the bellows, neither can the bellows work without the keyboards.

Unlike most other instruments, it is not possible for the accordionist to watch both hands play at the same time. There is simply too much distance between them. In a sense, each hand must trust that the other hand can do its part without being watched all the time. Each hand must learn to play the keyboard it is given. Each hand must remember to both play its own notes, and work together to keep air moving through the bellows. At times, the hands will be quite a long way apart, and at others as close as they can be, and both these positions are necessary.

As we wind up this part on staying connected, let me suggest that you spend some time deciding together just what comprises your bellows. Each of you has your own hand work to practice, but you'll need that commitment to your connection to be able to make music together. I call this the stuff that you can't, or really shouldn't, do with people other than your spouse. This is what breathes life into your day-to-day activities.

I think there are three essential points of contact, but you may find others that help move air through your marriage. The first of these is sex. As discussed in the last chapter, you will need to make a commitment to make sex work in your marriage, no matter how much effort it takes. It is just too important a matter to go unattended.

The second is a commitment to childcare and/or elder care. If you do not have a workable and flexible agreement for how you will raise children if or when you have them, or care for your parents in their aging if that responsibility falls to you, or how you will care for one another as you age and/or become unable to care for yourself in some way, these issues will not become problematic only when they actually arise, but will raise their anxious heads from the very beginning.

The third area is a commitment to each doing their part to keep the family moving forward in a commonly agreed upon direction. This is to say that it will be natural for there to be debates on how to get where you want to go, and variations in the capacity to contribute, but there should be no question as to your commitment to your destination (or at least the direction for now).

As I said, there may be other commitments that make up the core of your connectedness. But no matter what they are, they will leave you with plenty of freedom to explore the periphery without either of you feeling your bond threatened. Like the accordion, people may wonder how the two of you, so different in so many ways, so far apart at times and so close at others, could possibly make such beautiful music together, but you will know that your instrument works precisely because of its brilliant, if funny-looking, design.

QUESTIONS

How do you feel about the prospect of raising children, caring for an aging parent, or meeting the unexpected future needs of your spouse? How well prepared do you feel to do these things?

What is your destination or direction as a couple? How firm are your commitments to it?

How confident do you feel about your connection as a couple? About your ability to avoid overreacting when that connection feels more tenuous?

* * *

EXERCISE

Go to a solo accordion concert. It is not enough to watch on YouTube. This is something that really must be experienced live to appreciate fully.

PART 6

ESCAPE VELOCITY

As the old saying goes, all good things must come to an end, and that includes both your engagement and this book. You may now be just weeks or months from your wedding, and with a lot to do. In these pages, you have looked at how families generally function, and at how those dynamics often play out in the life of a newlywed couple. In this final part, I want to offer some final observations that I hope will pull everything together for you before you set off down the aisle.

There's an old true story about endings that goes like this. A couple had been meeting with their pastor before their wedding and it was time to wrap up. As was his custom, the pastor asked the couple if there was any last thing they wanted to ask their future spouse in the security of the pastor's presence. The bride had none, but the groom said, "Honey, it's really not a big thing, but I just want to know why you cut the ends off the ham before you cook it."

The bride replied that she had no idea why she always did that. It was just the way her family had always done it. But later at home, the question began to intrigue her, so she called her mother and asked her the same question. She received the same answer. Not satisfied, she then called her grandmother and posed the question. To which her grandmother replied, "Well, so it will fit into my roasting pan."

As has probably become clear by now with all the in-law examples I have used, there is a very powerful generational influence to your marriage, far deeper than kitchen traditions. If so minor a thing as cutting off the ends of a ham gets transmitted, how much more those truly defining characteristics of our families? I do not mean to suggest that your fate is sealed on the basis of your family's neuroses. Far from it. But I am suggesting that unless you look into it on that basis, you will struggle to understand what is going on in your own marriage.

Perhaps a helpful way to illustrate this is to return to that space-walking astronaut of the last chapter. He or she is not naturally a part of that hostile (or some would say peaceful) environment. That astronaut is an earth creature who has left earth. To leave earth, he or she needed to overcome gravity, and its companion laws of physics like dealing with inertia, opposite and equal reactions and all the rest. Those are clearly not insurmountable obstacles, but they do require sometimes extraordinary energy and effort to overcome.

It does not take much energy to leave the ground. You may not be able to slam dunk a basketball, but your body can briefly be suspended in midair by jumping. You have, in a sense, opposed gravity, at least for a moment before it reasserts itself. But if you want to leave the bonds of earth to venture into the stratosphere, you will need some greater source of energy, whether your vehicle is a hot air balloon or a jetliner. Eventually, however, both of these means of elevating your body will need to return to the ground when their energy supply runs out.

It is another story, however, in space. Once you break free from the earth's gravity, you can enter into orbit around the earth, rather than being stuck to it. You are still connected to earth, but it no longer requires as much energy to stay up high as it did with the balloon or jetliner. Like the moon, you can endlessly and economically circle around the planet, keeping it in view, communicating with it, maybe even receiving visitors from there. It is also possible to change your orbit in space, higher or lower in relation to earth, and doing so requires less energy than getting into orbit in the first place.

But first you have to get off the ground. I remember being fascinated learning in science class about rockets and "escape velocity," that speed necessary for a ship to leave earth's gravitational pull and enter into a higher orbit. Escape velocity may be a fixed speed, but each ship's needs must be calculated from known factors that include not only gravity, but also the thrust behind you and the weight of the ship. All of those factors require a delicate balancing act.

At the risk of stretching this metaphor too far, it is also possible to pass out of earth's orbit and into open space or even into the orbit of another celestial body, and from there, it is extremely hard to get back to earth if you want to. No one can help you out there.

All of this is to say that unless you decide to become "lost in space," you will always be affected in some way by the massive influence of your family. But this does not mean that your new partnership is earth-bound. How much you want to minimize your family's emotional pull, or take advantage of its emotional power to hold you in orbit is up to you, but you'll need to know how much energy (and imagination) is required to get you where you want to go (and just maybe back home again). You see, back home, there's ham without end. And it's one of your family's favorite dishes. Amen.

It is a big leap from ham in a pan to outer space, so let's return to earth and note that the ham story suggests more than just that powerful generational forces are at work. It also suggests that there are questions and topics that others cannot precisely anticipate for you.

As you come to the end of the more formal part of preparation for your marriage (because ultimately, you will always be learning on the job), this is also the moment for you to ask any last questions or raise any last concerns before you start your journey. I have offered a number of questions as conversation starters, but these may not be the most helpful questions for your relationship. If that's the case, let me suggest that you formulate some that do work for you before things really start to speed up. And they will speed up, maybe even to escape velocity.

PAIN, FEVER, AND BLOOD
ARE OUR FRIENDS

I t's a story I have heard far too often in my work: a person puts off going to the doctor, struggles silently and stoically for a long time, enduring great discomfort, only to finally be forced by excruciating pain or incapacity to seek medical attention. A diagnosis returns that concludes that if the patient had come in for treatment sooner, something relatively simple could have been done to prevent the patient's pain and suffering, if not save his or her life. Our health is nothing to trifle with.

Your goal for your marriage is likely the same as almost everyone else: to have a healthy marriage and family. "Healthy" is, of course, a sort of vague term that may call to mind images of physical fitness and bodily vitality, and those are pursuits certainly worth spending time on. But even before we begin to talk about emotional health, it is worth remembering a few things about that physical part of being human, namely that the presence of pain, fever, and blood is actually a good thing.

Pain, fever, and blood are the body's way of telling us that something is amiss. Although they are unpleasant, they are not something we should want to avoid entirely. It is not the pain, fever, and blood which are the body's problem. They are the body's response to a problem; their presence alerts us to find out why they have sounded the alarm. Then we can bring healing to a body that needs it, and avoid the kind of unnecessary tragedy with comes with ignoring or denying the symptoms.

121

Emotional pain works the same way. As with our bodies, the relationship warning signs of emotional pain, conflict, anguish, depression, and others alert us that something is not quite right, even if they do not tell us how severe is the underlying illness. Often, we are able to "treat" them with some tenderness, compassion, honesty, or directness, our doses of emotional aspirin or antibiotics.

But when they become more persistent or downright chronic, it is time to seek a more informed opinion. And there is absolutely no reason to wait until they are relationship-threatening. That is when they are the hardest to treat.

When you visit your doctor for a regular checkup, he or she evaluates you according to certain age-appropriate criteria such as height, weight, blood pressure, etc. There are some standards by which to measure your state of health. These exist for the state of your family's health too. Although they may be expressed differently by different people, here is one useful way to evaluate your relationship, based on the work of Peter Steinke:

- Healthy families accept differences
- Healthy families focus on strengths
- Healthy families focus on the future
- Healthy families deal appropriately with their anxiety

It should be clear to you by now how these are related to the overall themes of the book, and that they are markers of emotional maturity and self-differentiation. But knowing what describes health, and practicing it are, of course, two different things entirely. And so it takes some honesty about the presence of the warning signs to evaluate the health of your relationship.

If you find in either your marriage or your family of origin that you are beyond your own abilities to make progress in these areas, it is time to see some kind of marriage doctor, whether that be a psychologist, family therapist, member of the clergy, or even just a wise friend in whom you can confide in trust. (These are not, by the way, necessarily ranked in order of effectiveness.) It may be difficult to make that decision, but there is simply no reason to needlessly suffer or allow the condition to get worse.

There are many reasons why some people refuse to visit the doctor, none of them very compelling when weighed against the consequences for themselves and their families. Again, the same is true in our relationships, although it comes with even higher hurdles.

You see, our bodies are supposed to break down, eventually at least, but not our relationships. The vow reads, "till death do we part," not "till divorce do we part." We may feel shame, or fear judgment, in revealing we have an emotional issue we cannot handle or bear, that it suggests some kind of underlying character flaw or weakness. But of course, nothing could be further from the truth. We are in fact exhibiting the highest virtue of our character and our strength by seeking counsel from someone who can help us.

I often find that people perceive hospitals as places of sickness and death. But I find them to be places of life and healing. More people enter the hospital and leave healed than enter to suffer and die. Not all relationships can be saved by counseling, therapy, prayer, or wisdom, but very few die from them either. You'll never find out if you don't try. For all of our sakes, don't wait until it is too late.

QUESTIONS

How does your body "somatize" (react to) emotional discomfort, pain or stress? How do you know physically when you are feeling pressure?

Do you agree with the four indicators of healthy families? What else would you add? How might you put those in your own words?

How do you feel about the "helping professions"? Do you believe they have something to offer? If so, what? If, not, what are they lacking?

* * *

EXERCISE

Read about different approaches to helping troubled relationships and see which one(s) makes you most comfortable. Keep that info on hand just in case the need arises.

CLEARING UP STATIC

I f the popular media is to be believed, the most common ailment of marriages is bad communication between the partners: they don't have good listening skills, they don't share openly from the heart, there are gender differences that challenge them, among other short circuits. And if most marriage gurus are to be believed, better communication is the answer and they offer an endless variety of ways to improve a couple's communication. You might be tempted to think that this is a key element in the concept of "staying connected" I have been talking about. But it's not.

The main problem with this perspective is that it sends couples chasing after the Holy Grail of relationships. I've heard more than one couple in crisis say to me, "If only we communicated better, everything would be OK." They feel that if each person could just get their points across in way their partner could understand, they could move forward with greater harmony.

I'm never sure whether it is good news or not to tell them that they are actually communicating quite brilliantly, artistically even. They are sending their messages out loud and clear, and they are being received loud and clear. If they couldn't understand what the other one was communicating, they'd have no reason to fight. The fight starts when the communication takes place in an atmosphere of that pesky "morally neutral emotional stimulus that comes from a real or perceived threat," and they react instead of respond. The only couples that have communications problems are those that need a dictionary to translate from one language to another. The rest have anxiety problems.

I was once at a church meeting during which two opposing sides were trying to come to an understanding. Each presented their case quite clearly. Both sides could even repeat back quite well what their opponents had articulated. But they could get nowhere toward agreement because each side was simply reacting to what the other side had very clearly communicated. I could almost see a kind of emotional static hanging in the air between them preventing them from responding creatively to the abundant and genuinely helpful information each side had shared. They were not nearly as far from agreement as they thought. But they all left the way they had entered: anxious and feeling misunderstood.

This is why some people are very skilled at mediating conflicts. They do not simply rephrase or repackage what has been said. Instead, they are able to calm the parties down enough to address the substantive issues. They clear away the emotional static that does not allow us to process the shared communication in any helpful way.

What I am calling emotional static isn't necessarily the anxiety between two people. It is actually more likely to be anxiety coming from some other part of your life that is now interfering where it doesn't belong. Your spouse tries to relate an emotionally taxing event that happened at work that day, but try as you might, you just can't stay connected to the story, not because your spouse is not expressing it well or clearly, but because you just learned your best friend has cancer. Your spouse perceives that you are not really present, blames you for not listening, and the conflict takes on a life of its own. Neither of you has been able to take responsibility for your own emotions, either by declaring up front that hearing the story at another time would be preferable, or by not becoming defensive when the other person doesn't vibrate the way you want them too.

Maybe the bigger problem with blaming the communication issue is that focusing on bettering communication is directing energy and effort away from more significant issues. "Our communication issue" becomes part of a triangle that forces communication to be the topic of conversation, rather than what has really raised the anxiety of one or both of you.

Maybe you have seen people get frustrated trying to communicate with someone who speaks a different language. They begin to speak a-lot-more-slow-ly and a lot LOUDER, as if that would make a difference. This is the same approach most couples take when they fight. They repeat themselves and raise the volume. But this doesn't work any better in marriage than in a foreign country. Clearing up static takes a lot more work than enunciating more clearly and looking your partner in the eye.

It may be more helpful to think about this emotional static not as a fog that floats between two people keeping words and emotions from getting through, but more like that old image of the rain cloud that seems to hang over only one person's head. The static you need to clear up is the static your anxiety creates. Clearing it up helps make sure that the two clouds don't join together and start a storm that gets you both wet. Better for each of you to break out your own umbrellas and walk side-by-side having a nice, pleasant, anxiety-free conversation.

QUESTIONS

Can you identify static in other conversations or relationships you've had?

Can you describe a situation when someone's ability to stay calm moved the conversation forward?

Have you found "communication" or other couple's issues more easily the focus of your energy when you are anxious?

* * *

EXERCISE

Make a list of the words or phrases most likely to raise your anxiety in a conversation or argument. Share that list with your future spouse, but also start trying to disassociate those triggers from your partner.

It Really Does Take That Village

That old proverb that "It takes a village to raise a child" has taken a beating over the years. But being dissected or used as a political football doesn't make it any less valuable wisdom about childrearing or about keeping a marriage healthy.

Of course, villages are actually just really big families with the same kinds of issues as smaller families, but we'll pretend for the purpose of this chapter that the village in question is a pretty well-functioning family.

In a historical way, the proverb speaks to the reality I shared earlier about emotional health in generations past that depended more broadly on extended family, and other support networks rather than on the shoulders of a couple alone. No one can do it that way.

Of course, your village will not necessarily be geographically defined so much as pulled together from all the areas of your life—family, work, study, friends, religion, and others—that you have collected along the way. A good, solid sense of place never hurts, but it is not the most essential element.

It is in this village that you will grow, or stagnate, as a couple and as individuals depending on how well you avail yourself of what the community has to offer you, and how much you offer yourself to the community. As in responsibility taking of all kinds, you get out of something what you put into it.

I've alluded earlier to the need to not isolate yourselves, and to seek out help when you need it. But the village

129

offers you a kind of preventative care. Taking advantage of what the whole village has to offer is probably the easiest way to avoid a trip to the village doctor. The doc is not the only one who can offer up health and healing. It comes in a variety of forms from a wide group of people.

Here are some observations I've made over the years about our villages that may also be helpful for you:

In your village there are elders and teachers and artists, prophets and poets, mechanics and gardeners, eccentrics and outcasts. Each of them offers something you need to continue to grow in your sense of self and stay connected to others, whether or not it is obvious to you. Some of the best wisdom comes from the unlikeliest of places.

In your village, there are plenty of people who have failed at one thing or another, in their marriages and careers, as parents or citizens. Their pain and anger, as much as their humility and grace, have much to teach you.

In your village, there will be temptations. You will be enticed to gossip and slander, to degrade the environment, to hoard the gifts you have received, to believe no one can be trusted or that no one is really there for you.

In your village, you will trust people and they will betray you. Do not be disillusioned when they disappoint you or fail you. As with your spouse, your emotional well-being cannot be dependent on anyone else.

In your village you will be called upon to get involved, to go to town meetings and speak your piece (or peace), to raise a neighbor's barn, to bring over a casserole full of comfort food, to watch a single mother's children. These are the ways you pay your debt to the village, or give thanks for it.

In your village there will be natural disasters, chaos, and tragedy. You will learn in these times the strengths and weaknesses of not only your fellow villagers, but yourselves as well. You will see how you complement each other, and how vital each is to the next. And you will cherish that.

In your village, whether you do it well or poorly, your marriage will be a testimony to others, whether they are your children, or the newlyweds who just moved in next door. Each will have to take responsibility for themselves, but you will have helped or hindered them in the process.

In your village you will learn that it is the sum total of your life together that you can call happy, and less so the daily grind, but that this is good enough, and not worth get stressed about. You will learn how important it is to cultivate your own self so that your daily happiness is not dependent on the mood between you and your beloved.

Finally, in your village you will celebrate and learn the awful but beautiful truth that marriage is usually only "happily ever after" in retrospect, when you are sitting at a milestone anniversary and looking out over the guests that have come to celebrate you or when you are with old friends and they remember you "way back when" and their presence gives you permission to do the same for yourselves as a couple. And those celebrations let you see what "happily ever after" is all about.

QUESTIONS

What have been the key places or institutions in your village?

How connected do you feel to other parts of the village?

How do you hope to describe your "happily ever after" on your tenth or twentieth anniversary?

* * *

EXERCISE

If you will be moving together to a new place, check out what the "village" in your new community has to offer. If you are not moving, get to know those aspects of village life your future spouse finds important.

FLIGHT 2 NINER 7,
RUNWAY ONE EIGHT CENTER
IS NOW CLEARED FOR LANDING

Soon after your wedding, you may find yourselves on an airplane heading for your honeymoon. If you are lucky, someone will have sprung for first class, but either way, you will recline your seat after the recent weeks and months of activity, begin to unwind, and look forward to the beach or wherever you may have chosen to go.

You can do this comfortably because you are in good hands in the friendly skies. Your friendly air traffic controllers see to it that your flight takes off, gets where it is supposed to go, and lands safely. And they do it well. The old saying is true that the most dangerous part of your trip is the drive to the airport.

What you don't see while you are plugging in your headphones is the amazing amount of stress the men and the women in the airport towers are under. Being an air traffic controller has been rated as the most stressful of all jobs because they are responsible for thousands of lives at every moment of their workday.

But your plane is not going to crash. Very few do. That is because air traffic controllers know how to manage their anxiety and not freak out when they see two planes a little too close together on the radar. They know how to maintain a calm presence and tone of voice in the midst of pilots taxiing down the wrong runway, a baggage truck in the wrong place at the wrong time, or a landing gear that won't go down.

These air traffic controllers can teach us at least two things. The first is that you can (and indeed must) remain calm under pressure, whether at home, work, or church. Even when there is a great deal at stake, it is possible to keep it from turning into chaos. The essential task is to maintain your composure.

The other is related to just how these air traffic controllers can do this, namely that they can see the bigger picture–literally. Up in the tower, and with their radar, they can see the whole airport's organized complexity much more clearly than a pilot in a cockpit or baggage handler on the tarmac. They can see that the planes really aren't as close together as the pilots think they are, that the weather patterns aren't as never-ending as the passengers feel them to be. From their view from up top, they have a better feel for the system and how it works. And from that perspective, it's a lot easier to not panic no matter how much activity is going on.

When you can begin to understand more clearly how each of your own families work (including yourselves, of course), you will feel more like the controller in the tower than the passenger in the midst of turbulence. You will be able to see the ways your family members behave like the takeoffs and landings of aircraft—the very purpose of an airport—scheduled but with the possibility of delay, subject to pilot error and even crashes, but more or less predictable and manageable and therefore not worth getting quite so stressed about.

Of course, let me be very clear that you are not the controller. It is not your job to direct anyone's behavior or tell anyone what to do. Your job is simply to be as calm and composed as a real controller no matter what is going on around you. This view from above is an exalted position only because of the perspective it gives you, not because it gives you any power over anyone else. If there is any power involved, it is the power of self-control you can more easily exercise because you aren't taken by surprise when someone begins to triangle you, or pursue you. You experience control when you don't feel the need to overreact when someone blames or criticizes you. This self-control is possible because you know these things are as regular and inevitable as the departures and arrivals at your local airport.

As unpredictable as families sometimes seem, their behavior is actually quite predictable, especially over time. Relationships develop rigid patterns that are difficult to change when we can't see the bigger picture. In the midst of a shouting match, we perceive it as a personality conflict between two people rather than as part of the way a bigger system has helped shape us to interact with one another. When we can step back and gain some perspective, we can begin to change our roles in a relationship and begin to create a healthier pattern.

Once your real air traffic controllers have done their jobs and you are safely home from your honeymoon, you might find it useful to begin to map out your families' systems, and to begin to see the patterns that have formed over generations, and that still play a role today in how your family members relate to one another. One such tool for doing this is a genogram, a kind of emotional family tree, which helps us understand our relationships. This may help you appreciate the bigger picture of your family the way those controllers do of their airports.

QUESTIONS

How do you experience your family as a whole? Do you feel like the passenger in the plane, or the person in the tower?

What has helped you in the past as a means to self-control? Do you think that is enough? Will you need other tools?

Can you identify some of the patterns, or scripts, you have developed with your future spouse or other family members?

***

EXERCISE

Create a genogram of your family. (Information on how to create a genogram is widely available on the Internet).

FROM NEWLYWED TO FOREVERWED

After months of planning, and much agonizing over details like the borders of napkins, bridesmaids' dresses, and hors d'oeuvres, the big day finally arrived.

I stepped into the church just before the time announced for the ceremony and found exactly one couple seated in the pews. What nerve, I thought, showing up late for someone's wedding!

At the same time, my wife was discovering that her sister had been left behind at the hairdresser, some twenty minutes away. Someone was dispatched to pick her up.

Meanwhile at the site of the reception, the caterer was reattaching the top part of our cake that had fallen over in the August heat, and was carefully disguising the scar with wildflowers.

It wasn't quite a full-blown fiasco but it was all stressful enough that by the time my wife was ready an hour later to walk down the aisle, she was about to become a tearful wreck, in the wrong sort of way. But then experience and grace blessedly intervened.

As the wedding march began, she looked up ahead and caught the steely gaze of the wise and experienced minister who was marrying us. She reports with gratitude that he gave her a look that simultaneously communicated that she really needed to pull it together right away or risk spoiling the moment, and also that everything was going to be just fine.

And so, with a final sniff, she joined me up front and we got married in a ceremony for which we were both fully present. Everyone had arrived, including her sister. We enjoyed the reception with our family and friends, no one was ever the wiser on the damaged cake, and we even survived a lurid display by one of the groomsmen who got carried away during the garter game.

But that was just what was happening on the surface.

Behind the scenes, a family crisis was playing out as a key member of my wife's family lay on death's doorstep. Her grandmother, who had traveled a long distance for the wedding, stayed back with a few other family members to be with him. He died the following day, having waited, we choose to believe, so as not to spoil our special day.

In the congregation that day were people whose own marriages were already dissolving, or who came to that day with strained relationships with other guests.

I was baptized in the very chapel in which our wedding took place. The organist, who for years had been a father figure to me, was retiring and playing his final wedding. My own father played the violin, my brother sang, my future sister-in-law read a poem, with each person bringing their own form of performance anxiety.

There will always be so much more going on at your wedding and in your marriage than meets the eye. And it will all generate anxiety, both the good kind and the not-so good kind, that may find you from time to time about to become a tearful wreck in the wrong sort of way, the way that causes you to miss out on what is special about your life. But you can pull yourself together and know that everything will be OK.

As most brides and grooms learn, even the most carefully planned wedding rarely goes as planned. And that is just one day. You can plan for a lot of things, even in a marriage, but you cannot plan for everything. Nevertheless, you can be a lot more prepared to deal with those things you didn't plan for (and those things for which your original plan was inadequate!) and that will make all the difference.

My hope is that this book has been like the look in our minister's eye that helps you start to be fully present in all the ups and downs of your marriage, from the day of your wedding ceremony until the very end. Saying "I do" with your eyes wide open about who you are and where you come from is the best way I know of going from newlywed to foreverwed, and having a marriage that will be a blessing to you and to everyone else as well.

No More Questions or Exercises!

Go get married, you crazy kids!

ABOUT THE AUTHOR

Stacey Steck grew up in Cleveland Heights, Ohio and has lived and traveled in many places since. He is a graduate of the American University in Washington D.C. and Pittsburgh Theological Seminary, and is currently a student at Pfeiffer University. He has been a Presbyterian pastor since 2000, serving churches in St. Cloud, Minnesota, San José, Costa Rica, and Salisbury, North Carolina. In that time, he has offered pre-marital counseling to dozens of couples, as well as counseling, coaching, and spiritual direction to many more individuals, couples, and families.

43798313R00084

Made in the USA
Middletown, DE
19 May 2017